ENDOR

GARY GROGAN I.E, PAPA G – Go2020
Director – Legacy Pastor of Stone Creek Church – Board Member of North Central University – Regional Presbyter of the Central Region of Illinois District of Assemblies of God – Spiritual father.

Philip Shorey is someone most people have never heard of. He is not famous, but he is an artist and composer, a very creative person, and a messenger for Jesus. Where Philip goes, most of us will probably never go. He is a true evangelist to the forgotten, outliers, and those on the fringes of society. He tells stories about Jesus through his traveling marionette theatre called *The Suitcase Sideshow*. He ministers in homeless shelters, slums, refugee camps, brothels, orphanages, anarchist theaters, and street corners all over America and the world. I have witnessed him firsthand minister on the streets of New Orleans during Mardi Gras with our ministry, *Answering the Cries*. People listen and get saved.

His book *Travelogues of a Family Sideshow* demonstrates the power of story. It is a captivating narrative of a modern-day indigenous messenger of Jesus Christ full of real and miraculous stories. As a child and teenager, I read and re-read the missionary stories of Victor Plymire in Tibet, Jim and Elizabeth Elliot in Ecuador, Lillian Trasher in Egypt, Mark and Huldah Buntain in India, and many others. Just as those true stories impacted my life and ministry so many years ago, so the true stories in *Travelogues of a Family Sideshow* have affected me at this stage of my life to reach more people for Jesus.

Philip is not a flash in the pan. His family traces back to four generations of ministers that have been effective in soul-winning ministry. He started doing ministry as a child and now teaches his own three children, along with his wife Sari, to do the

I

same. Very few today demonstrate this type of dedication in our western culture that worships comfort and ease. I love reading stories filled with biblical truth and personal testimonies by real followers of Jesus. The greatest thing I could say about Philip Shorey is that he is an authentic follower of Jesus.

———————◆———————

DAVID WILSON – Founder – TACO International

Family legacies are a dime a dozen. There are the Kahns (Genghis and company), the Kardashians, and the Windsors (The Royal Family) among many famous and well-known families. Very, very few will have heard of the Shorey Family or Rasmussen Clan...except in the unseen realm. As Philip says early on in his book when confronted with a Maori gang of prisoners and feeling God speaking to him, "Yes, they won't listen to you, but they will listen to me and I'm going to use you to do that." God ESPECIALLY uses the weak and humble and there are few books you will read where several generations of a family accomplish more in that realm. It has been a privilege for our teams in Turkey, Bulgaria, and Kyrgyzstan to be a recipient of this family legacy and also to be part of the legacy by Philip and Sari helping us form Suitcase Sideshow 2.0 that continues to be used around Turkey and Bulgaria.

———————◆———————

DUSTIN KELM – Founder – Unishow

After roaming the world for a few decades myself as an evangelizing performing spectacle, I relished Philip's powerful account of how God can move in unexpected ways when we step out in faith, boldness, and obedience. This book reveals how our every decision matters, not just for today but for generations with far reaching eternal impact as we surrender each stage of life to Him. Through this captivating ancestral journey, we see the bigger picture of how God is at work and the incredible things He will do when we say, "YES!" to Jesus and let Him work through us in ways beyond our imagination or scope.

DAVID PIERCE – Founder – Steiger International

If you want to discover what it means to live a life of faith and courage. Read this book. If you long to experience what you read about in the book of Acts. This book is for you. If you don't want to be challenged and stay comfortable. This book is not for you!!!

————————◆————————

CHAD JOHNSON – Founder – Come&Live! – former A&R of Tooth and Nail Records

Philip's passion for street storytelling is intriguing, lively and otherworldly. His desire to see Jesus made famous—in places and to people who likely will never hear the gospel story as he is gifted to tell it—is refreshing of the tallest order. This book is a powerful resource to any artistically- wired follower of Jesus seeking to engage culture way outside the four walls of church. Any artist willing to kill their art is ultimately the hero for recognizing gift is never higher than giver. God doesn't need more gifted creatives to show off skill, He's seeking a generation willing to surrender everything (including the very gift they've been given). Philip qualifies as dangerous soul with a sharp story to tell in *Travelogues of a Family Sideshow*.

TRAVELOGUES OF A FAMILY SIDESHOW

PHILIP SHOREY

steiger press

Travelogues of a Family Sideshow

Published by Steiger Press,
PO Box 236
Wheaton, IL 60187-0236
www.steiger.org
intoffice@steiger.org
www.suitcasesideshow.org

Travelogues of a Family Sideshow/ Philip Shorey. – 1st ed.

ISBN 978-0-9978649-4-6

VIII

IN LOVING MEMORY OF

MARILYN LOIS RASMUSSEN

1935 - 2013

Storyteller, prayer warrior, historian,
massage therapist, photographer, piano
teacher, performer, worship leader,
figure skater, gardener, adventure seeker,
missionary, competitor, pastor's wife,
mother, grandmother, great-grandmother,
daughter, and writer.

x

"In a time not that long ago, though, people with extreme physical abnormalities were not only considered as "freaks" or "monstrosities" by society at large, but they sometimes were ostracized even by their own families. The **sideshow** was just about the single institution that was welcoming of one who was born with, say, four legs or perhaps with no legs. The **sideshow** not only presented these social outcasts with the chance to earn a living, but it also gave them an opportunity to interact with others, and sometimes even find **love**."[a]

THE RINGLING BROTHERS AND BARNUM & BAILEY CIRCUS

CONTENTS

OCEAN
Beaufort Sea
Baffin Bay
Gulf of Alaska
Hudson Bay
Labrador Sea
CANADA
NORTH AMERICA
UNITED STATES
Seattle
Portland
San Francisco
Dallas
Houston
New York
Philadelphia
Boston
Gulf of Mexico
Havana
Mexico City
Caribbean Sea
Caracas
VENEZUELA
COLOMBIA
ECUADOR
PERU
BOLIVIA
PARAGUAY
CHILE
PACIFIC
.1
.2
.3
.4
.5
.6
.7
.8
.9
.10
.11
.12
.13
.14
.15
.16
.17
.18
.19
.20
.21
.22
.23
.24
.25
.26
.27
.28
.56
.57

1. Minto, Alaska	20. Saskatoon, Canada	39. Lubiąż, Poland
2. Ketchikan, Alaska	21. Rossland, Canada	40. Swinoujscie, Poland
3. Klukwan, Alaska	22. Burnaby, Canada	41. Wrocław, Poland
4. Tacoma, Washington	23. Kootenay, Canada	42. Warsaw, Poland
5. Reedsport, Oregon	24. Regina, Canada	43. Krakow, Poland
6. Los Angeles, California	25. Kimberly, Canada	44. Budapest, Hungary
7. Kansas City, Missouri	26. Osoyoos, Canada	45. Debrecen, Hungary
8. Denver, Colorado	27. Montreal, Canada	46. Miskolc, Hungary
9. New Orleans, Louisiana	28. Québec, Canada	47. Marghita, Romania
10. Minneapolis, Minnesota	29. São Paulo, Brazil	48. Bucharest, Romania
11. Grand Forks, North Dakota	30. South Hampton, Ireland	49. Constanta, Romania
12. Chester New, Hampshire	31. Liverpool, England	50. Istanbul, Turkey
13. Derry New, Hampshire	32. Give Vejle, Denmark	51. Diyarbakır, Turkey
14. Ellsworth, Maine	33. Karlstad, Sweden	52. Kiev, Ukraine
15. Saugas, Massachusetts	34. Bern, Switzerland	53. Sumy, Ukraine
16. Winnipeg, Canada	35. Berlin, Germany	54. Moscow, Russia
17. Calgary, Canada	36. Krögis, Germany	55. Bishkek, Kyrgyzstan
18. Vancouver, Canada	37. Prague, Czech Republic	56. Wellington, New Zealand
19. Lethbridge, Canada	38. Poznan, Poland	57. Auckland, New Zealand

ACKNOWLEDGMENTS

TRAVELOGUES OF A FAMILY SIDESHOW is the response to an idea that repeated over and over. Around the dinner table with family and around the world with people I had just met—I kept hearing "Wow, you should write a book," and "That story sounds like a movie." Eventually the idea started to take root. This book has been a dream for many in the family over the last century, and it is an honor to bring it to completion. To all of those who subtly influenced this work to take place, I thank you.

To all of those who have had a part in making this book possible, I thank you. To my loving wife Sari, for making these adventures a reality, who has sacrificed so much, and is an inspiration to me, I thank you. To my kids, Axel, Casper, and Juneau—for their patience in my writing process, I thank you. To Leanor Ortega-Till for being such a friend and guide to my creative and spiritual endeavors, I thank you. To David Pierce for being an inspiration and spiritual father, I thank you. To Mark Anderson (Q) for being a servant-hearted genius, I thank you. To Felipe Rocha, for your friendship and creative calling to serve and reach the lost with your art, I thank you. To all the many people who have traveled with The Suitcase Sideshow over many continents and through many uncertainties, I thank you. To Mark Johnson for healing my perspective of church, I thank you. To Sally Grayson for being such a musical inspiration, friend, and support in all your wild, creative ways, I thank you. For Russel Munson for your continued partnership in the arts, I thank you. To Wes Halula for your creative inspiration and mentoring, I thank you. To my mom and dad, John and Shawnette Shorey, for your love, sacrifice, and for instilling a passion for God by example, I thank you. To my father and mother-in-law, Mark and Jill Schwarzbauer, for being a blessing, encouragement, and being a part of my family story, I thank you. To Edgar and Patti Rasmussen for your life, joy, and inspiration, I thank you. To all of our supporters and friends who have partnered with us in this adventure, I thank you. To Brad Rasmussen, Brenda Lukinuk, Kyle Rasmussen, Craig Rasmussen, and all the rest of the family, for your love, support, prayers, research, and willingness to journey with me and work on this together—I THANK YOU.

Accompanying Writers:
Aksel Rasmussen, Marilyn Rasmussen,
John Shorey, and Sari J. Shorey

Artwork:
Sally Grayson

Creative Editors:
Leanor Ortega-Till and Sari J. Shorey

Editor:
Celinda Olive

Creative Director:
Felipe Rocha

FOREWARD

By **LEANOR ORTEGA-TILL** *– Five Iron Frenzy*

A FAMILY IS fluid. It has several members each with particular callings, challenges and curses. Sometimes families experience generational callings. Meet the curious family of Philip Shorey. A family of immigrants, widows and widowers, at times poverty stricken and often misunderstood. When their road became difficult, rather than fussing and complaining with God they chose time and time again to call out to others to share the story of God's provision and goodness to them. It is this childlike faith perhaps that led them to tap into creativity and wonder as they cultivated their gifts for evangelism through puppetry.

TRAVELOGUES OF A FAMILY SIDESHOW

PROLOGUE

TRAVELOGUES OF A FAMILY SIDESHOW is an altar for remembering all that God has done through five generations of a family. The history of every travelogue has been thoroughly researched through the Give Museum in Denmark, history books, ancestral records, journals, comparisons of family accounts, and interviews. Not every miracle and misery is documented in this book and it is a fraction of what this family has seen God do. In a similar manner, we can't know everything Christ did on earth. If you recall:

"Jesus did many other things as well. If every one of them were written down, I suppose that even the whole world would not have room for the books that would be written." - JOHN 21:25

By the example of Noah, Abraham, Jacob, and many others; when God does the impossible, we need to do something to never forget it. In ancient times, they stacked rocks, built altars, worshiped God, and they left them there for future generations as a reminder of God's goodness. This book is also an altar to remember that with God, an extraordinary and unimaginable life is possible. (Matthew 19:26)

As a small disclaimer, the following writings could lead the reader to be overly impressed by this family, and as a result be under impressed with God's mercy. You are about to read how God has used five generations to impact the world for Jesus through the arts, and one could think, "Wow, what a family, they must have parenting down perfectly to pass this heart and legacy down through their family tree." As it is true that

God has blessed this family with wonderful kids and wisdom in raising them, it is also true that it would be a mistake to think that this family is perfect and has had no problems. Rather, let this book be a monument to God's mercy for all families and individuals who simply say, "Yes" to Christ's leading, from the prisoner to the pastor. It doesn't take a perfect person to allow a generational blessing to flourish, but one full of a humble surrendering of their plans, desires, and ambitions. One who is willing to be molded by the work of the Holy Spirit and put everything on the line for the call of God.

"Know therefore that the Lord your God is God; he is the faithful God, keeping his covenant of love to a thousand generations of those who love him and keep his commandments."

- DEUTERONOMY 7:9

The following pages feature that story through the origins of each generation of the Rasmussen Clan. As this story passes through history, it encounters some of the century's most notable events; including the sinking of the *Titanic*, the Great Depression, World Wars, 9/11, the effects of the internet, the collapse of the 35W bridge in Minneapolis, and the Coronavirus. After an introduction to each generation you will read spotlight stories shared from their musings and journals for a closer look into their faith, life in their era, and their perspective. From an anthropologist perspective of the arts and culture, I invite you to take note on how the language of the Gospel, culture, and the arts change from generation to generation.

As I wrote this book it added to my faith in the firsthand biblical accounts of those who wrote the Bible, because when you see God move, you remember. Even years later, you remember like it was yesterday because it changes you and makes an impression on your heart.

.

PRISON CAMP
KARAOKE

(2008)

MANY YEARS AGO I performed a simple puppet show at a prison camp for notorious gang members. How did I arrive at such a unique activity? Well, I met a New Zealander while in Germany in 2006, and he encouraged me to visit his country by saying, "If you ever come to New Zealand, I'll set up a tour for you in the North Island." Two and a half years later, I was traveling through New Zealand with my marionette street theater, The Suitcase Sideshow. As I crossed through the land of Middle Earth, I hitched a ride with a truck driver just past Mordor and eventually arrived at the grassy battlefields of Pelennor[1] near the Kapti Coast. Mid-trip the driver pulled off the road and wanted my traveling partner and me to get out of his truck in the desert. I became worried that this strange person would either shoot or abandon us. We got out but cautiously stayed in arms reach to the passenger door. The driver told us to smile and took our picture. In the end, praise Jesus, it was just an awkward photo-op.

Other than that brush with fear of being deserted in the desert, most of the tour was great. Our performance venues in New Zealand had included street corners, churches, and bars, but now it was time to visit a prison camp where none of the prisoners were interested in our show. It was a camp ran by Christians and the arrangement was that these big Maori felons could either do four years of hard time in prison, or only two years at a Christian camp. So despite their hate for Christians, they thought that it was a good deal and suffered through it. Now, to make their prison sentences even more grueling—they

1 For all of the non-geek readers, Mordor and the Pelennor Fields is in Middle Earth. It is the realm in which the book *The Lord of the Rings* takes place. It was filmed in New Zealand.

had to sit and watch a little puppet show.

We set up our stage, which is an old steamer trunk that transforms into a mini theater, and as I saw the brawny prisoners stroll in I confided to my tour manager, "I don't know what to say to these guys. I'm a skinny white kid from America with puppets. Why would these big Maori gang members even give me the time of day?" He told me, "Well first of all, they have no choice. Secondly, you should tell them what you told me about your family and the calling you have through the generations. Tell them about being the fourth generation to use puppets to share the Gospel. Show them that you use your grandparents' marionettes from the 1960's. Family honor and the shame they feel is a real big thing around here. That might impact them even more than your show." At that moment I felt God speaking to me, "Yes, they won't listen to you, but they will listen to me and I'm going to use you to do that."

The temptation in these kinds of situations is to act tough to win their respect by proving that you are a hardened dude that they can relate to. But that wasn't me. I don't have a crazy testimony of how Jesus saved me from drugs and got a hold of me in prison. I'm not hard or scary (except to maybe a little kid who once had nightmares about creepy marionettes after seeing my show and then told his mom he wanted to receive Jesus). I wasn't going to impress these guys, and I wasn't going to be a poser and try.

It wasn't me they needed to be impressed with anyway, but the power of God—the power that transformed the life of Saul, a murderer, and changed him into the Paul who wrote much of the New Testament. These guys needed the power that healed the sick, loved the unlovable, and defeated death on the cross. They needed the power that had started a generational blessing in my family over a hundred years ago with one man saying, "Yes" to Jesus after seeing The Salvation Army marching band in the park. This power revealed to me that I wasn't the black sheep of my family but right in line with a generational blessing if I would also say, "Yes" to God's calling. That same power could start a generational blessing in the lives and families of these hardcore criminals as well, if they would just say, "Yes" to Jesus and allow God to destroy the generational curse that was wasting their lives.

I had seen this common need all over the world; in places such as post-communistic countries, where they don't have past generations of people who had followed Jesus due to the political promotion of atheism, and camps in the Black Forest for orphans who felt cursed and disconnected from any honorable legacy. We all need to realize the generational blessing that is waiting around the corner once we join the family of God—not a blessing of ordinary wealth that fades and crumbles—but an eternal blessing of an extraordinary life founded on God's life-changing power that is available and undiscriminating for *all* people. Those are the shoulders we have the privilege to stand on.

This story of how God works through the generations is one that needs to be heard all over the world. It speaks to the lost children chasing meaning for their lives in all the wrong places. It speaks to the inner fabric of the human condition that longs for a heritage of honor.

Soon after the performance at the prison camp a beautiful and divinely orchestrated way to escape from a generational curse was offered to everyone. You could almost touch the Holy Spirit through how people were being moved in the room. I knew it wasn't the puppet show that did this and it wasn't my art, music, or a strange spell being transmitted through my antique relics. It was Jesus! Everyone, including the biggest guys with the most facial tattoos, prayed together for Jesus to come into their lives and change them that night. After that experience we enjoyed a bonding camaraderie brought on by their favorite activity: singing karaoke. When my turn came I belted out *Ring of Fire* by Johnny Cash.

GENERATION 1

IT WAS SPRING of 1910 and the end of the second wave of the Danish emigration to North America.[b] Johannes, breadwinner of the Rasmussen family, left the town of Give,[2] Denmark with his eldest son Alfred, to seek work and benefits from the government of Canada which was offering free land to new homesteaders. As a blacksmith, farmer, and inventor by trade, Johannes was strong with his hands and it is likely that he and his son worked as sailors on a ship across the Atlantic Ocean. His youngest daughter, Hilda (age 3), gave him her favorite teddy bear and informed him, "You can give it back to me when I see you again."

After arriving in Spring Coulee of Alberta, Canada and building a two-room home next to his new blacksmith shop, Johannes sent word for his wife Marie and the rest of the Rasmussen Clan to begin the long, difficult journey. With her wits and an unwavering backbone, Marie led the family, including no less than five children, across the North Sea from the port city of Esbjerg, Denmark, to the docks of South Hampton, England.

Before they departed Denmark, a man named Martin Clausen requested permission to marry Marie's eldest daughter, Laura. Marie had rescued him from the streets as part of a Lutheran-led alcohol prohibition in Denmark. He was living in her boarding house that assisted people as they withdrew from their addictions and destructive lifestyle. When he made his intentions known about her daughter and asked to marry her, Marie gave him a swift answer, "No, we're leaving for Canada." But, as the proverb of Song of Solomon says, "Many waters

---

2 Aksel was born in Brande, but lived above the blacksmith shop on Allégade which is now the Tunnellen Diskotek in Give. This was right before his father left for North America with Alfred.

cannot quench love; rivers cannot sweep it away."[3] Martin would not be swayed. He left his homeland and followed the family the entire journey as a single traveling man with no guarantees of what the future would hold.

There was word of a mighty ship that was departing soon from South Hampton, and the opportunity to board there and voyage to North America—more quickly than they previously planned—might be possible. This great ship was called the *RMS Titanic.*

Marie was only a nominal Lutheran at the time, as Lutheranism was Denmark's official state religion, yet she still felt it to be a bad omen when she saw a sign posted in front of the luxurious ocean liner that boasted, "Not even God himself could sink this ship!"[4] So despite having tickets in hand, Marie kicked the supreme confidence of humanity to the wayside and informed her children, "We will not take this ship, we will wait for the next one."

Had those traveling Rasmussens set foot on that historic vessel, this story most likely would have halted to a tragic end, sinking to the bottom of the North Atlantic. Possibly, there was a hand of protection for those who would not submit to the arrogance of man on that day. On April 15, 1912, after hitting an iceberg east of Nova Scotia, the *Titanic* sank into the Atlantic Ocean taking two thirds of its passengers and crew to the icy waters below.[c] The Rasmussen family instead exchanged their tickets and boarded a different White Star Line ship called the *SS Laurentic,*[5] which sailed across the Atlantic from Liverpool to Québec City. They passed over the Great Banks where

---

3 Song of Solomon 8:7

4 The sign quoting "Not even God himself could sink this ship!" has been disputed throughout the 20th century whether or not it actually ever existed. As for our story, this is how it was passed down through the generations, and was the given reason for why the Rasmussens did not board the Titanic.

5 During World War I, the *SS Laurentic* became a war vessel carrying solders and prisoners back and forth from Canada and West Africa to Liverpool. In 1917 the ship was blown up by two mines positioned by a German U-80 submarine sinking it to the bottom of the Irish Sea loaded with 43 tons of gold.

the *Titanic* was swallowed by icy waters, but saw no sign of remaining bodies or wreckage. It's easy to imagine the solemn chills of gratitude they would have felt while passing over this watery grave.[d]

Unfortunately, tragedy would still befall their journey. When the family arrived in Québec City on August 10, 1912, they took a transcontinental train to Lethbridge, Alberta where they were greeted by Alfred and an uninvited stranger. Together they led the family to Spring Coulee and the new house that Johannes had built, but he was not home. He had become very busy with work inventing farm equipment. He brought one of his new ideas to Montana, hoping to generate extra income, but while there his appendix burst. He was admitted to the hospital to have it removed but died of influenza and complications of the surgery on September 12, 1912.[6] The uninvited stranger was his undertaker who had come up from Montana to collect payment for Johannes' burial. When the family later traveled to Montana, they found his grave on a hilltop beneath a tree. It is said that young Hilda handled the loss of her father especially hard.

The family was in ruins. They had been miraculously saved by not boarding the *Titanic*, but now Marie was devastated and left to raise six children: Alfred, Trier, Sophus, Aksel, Laura, and Hilda—in a new land established by her late husband and without much at all.[7] Religion aside, they needed another miracle.

It became the responsibility of the boys to find work and provide for the rest of the family (in addition to funding a weekly poker game for themselves). The sons tried their best to keep up the homestead their father had built. They bought a cow

---

6 Father Johannes Fredrick Rasmussen (1863-1912), son of Johan Rasmussen and Sophie Rasmussen nee Hansen.

7 Alfred Møller Rasmussen (1889-1939), Andreas Anton Trier Rasmussen (1894-1955), Johannes Sophus Rasmussen (1894-1894, Twin to Andreas and died at birth), Aksel Johannes Rasmussen (1899-1983), Sophus Johannes Julius Rasmussen (1896-1941), Laura Rasmussen (1898-1995), Hilda Kathrine Sofie Rasmussen (1907-2010).

and searched for work, but life deep in the country was tough without much knowledge of the language and culture. With no resources, they were forced to move into Lethbridge, the neighboring town. There The Salvation Army was able to meet some of their practical needs and get this fatherless family on their feet.

Aksel was the youngest of the four boys and he changed his name to Alex to assimilate into the new country. Luckily for Alex, he found a friend named Edgar to teach him English so he was able to obtain a job delivering shoes by bicycle. Alex was good with his hands, always known as a clever and crafty fellow, and readily learned to ride a bicycle in the lane moments before the shoe delivery interview. This work supported the family. He did very well, received a promotion, and was soon learning how to repair shoes in the shop, which paid him $7.00 a week. This was good pay in the early 1900s! Then something special happened that would define his life forever.

Around the age of 16, Alex was walking in the park when he heard a marching band. He got a little closer and discovered it was The Salvation Army. Alex was so delighted by the music that he rounded up his friend Bill Rehorchuk, and they followed the marching band to the site of The Salvation Army's meeting one Sunday morning. Although Alex had grown up with a general notion of God in Denmark, he had never experienced Him in a tangible way for himself, but this time something was different. Seeds of hope had been planted through their ministy six years prior and now the timing was right. During that meeting Alex was filled with so much joy that he decided to say, "YES" to Jesus.

Alex joined The Salvation Army and knew that nothing was more important than to live a devoted life for Christ and in service to other people so that they may know Jesus too. This decision initially resulted in a falling out with his other brothers over their weekly poker night; however, the brothers eventually forgave Alex and joked that now they would win because they had someone praying for them!

It was God's use of The Salvation Army community that sustained the family and kept them afloat when the icebergs of settling into a new land were too immense to maneuver. Over time the whole family joined the movement and Alex entered The Salvation Army College in Winnipeg, Manitoba in the year of 1917. His enrollment in seminary turned out to be the very thing that kept him from being drafted into service during World War I. In those days, seminary students were able to opt out of military service in Canada. For Alex, this affirmed God's call on his life in knowing that God had spared him from active military duty. So, he took the call to ministry very seriously.

In 1929, the Great Depression hit. It was a wretched time for everyone. Alex was now fully enlisted in The Salvation Army as an officer who was stationed throughout Saskatchewan and Manitoba where he served by feeding the hungry and leading people to Jesus in their most desperate hour—sometimes even at his own expense. Once, in a hungry and malnourished condition, Alex phoned his mother to inform her of his tragic situation. Marie, having served in similar social care work in Denmark, and as a strong level-headed woman, assured him that he was "no good helping others if he didn't help himself as well." His mother suggested he eat some of the food he was giving out. She was always a source of stability and sound perspective.[8]

The Salvation Army took Alex all over Canada. One time, Alex participated in a conference and helped paint a house as a community service project. He was perched on a ladder when his eyes landed on the face of a lovely woman named Lavina Mae Fern Morrison. He did a double take when he saw her walk by, all the while still on the ladder, and then proceeded to literally fall for her! Fern (called by her second middle name

---

8 Laurine Marie Rasmussen nee Madsen (1866-1931), daughter of Anders Madsen and Ane Rasmussen nee Christensen, passed away in Calgary, Alberta, on April 23, 1931, shortly before Edgar was born. Being such a fighter, she had a private struggle with cancer and near the end of her battle, would often cough up blood and bury it in the basement dirt floor of the home she rented. Once her kids found out and got her a doctor, it was too late. The matriarch of the Rasmussen Clan, who saved her family from the *Titanic*, is buried in the Calgary, Alberta, Burnsland Cemetery (Lot; 166, Block; 9, Section; H,). "Never will your memory fade."

by all) was also a Captain in The Salvation Army. They married in 1930 and she birthed their first child, a son named Edgar, in 1932. Two years later, the couple welcomed their daughter Eunice to the family. Alex promised Fern never to speak Danish in her presence so she would never feel excluded from family conversations. He also promised God never to speak Danish again if God would answer his prayer to speak better English.

While the Great Depression was dragging on, and as their family grew, two of Alex's favorite pastimes became marching in The Salvation Army Band as a horn player and hosting street corner meetings proclaiming the gospel of Jesus Christ. He loved including his entire family whenever possible. Together they would sing to people walking by and often shared a message of true hope with struggling alcoholics. The family also hosted Bible studies to offer solid biblical answers to those spiritually seeking.

While the effects of the Great Depression continued to wreak havoc on the economy, Alex was determined to succeed. He had been working as a cobbler in Hudson's Bay Company in Calgary, Alberta, but was transferred to Winnipeg, Manitoba.

In addition to his skillful workmanship, Alex was also an unstoppable evangelist during work hours. His constant singing and sharing about Jesus got Alex into trouble. Once another employee become so frustrated with this behavior that he used a knife to cut up the shoe that Alex was repairing! It became clear to Alex that the solution, though a risky one, was to open up his own shoe repair shop. He did so in Winnipeg, Manitoba, and named it *Okay Repair Shop.* The store also sold cow horns which he crafted into lamps, salt and pepper shakers, cribbage boards, sailboats, bookends, vases and nightlights. Alex also started to repair many additional items including purses and umbrellas. The services they provided had to be greatly varied because income was fickle during this time of economic struggle. To draw the attention of people walking by, the shop window displayed an albino rat[9] and a big sign that read, "We

---

9 Oddly enough in 2008 CTV News reported that the invasive breed of albino rats

fix everything but broken hearts." Alex's son Edgar began a cobbler apprenticeship under his father at the *Okay Repair Shop* and the family of four resided in a rented apartment at the back of the store.[10]

For several years Alex continued working in his shoe shop, at times working full-time and at other seasons part-time, but he always managed to make time for his main passion of sharing the message of Jesus' love while working with The Salvation Army.

In 1946, he sold the *Okay Repair Shop* and moved his family to Vancouver in a black 1932 Studebaker and bought a house for $5,000. In this new city Alex was once again working with a Salvation Army mission; however, The Salvation Army was becoming more focused on social work. This didn't bother Alex, but he felt God leading him to join a pentecostal church because their beliefs and action were more evangelistic and in line with his gifting and calling. He yearned to use his creativity for God's glory and to share God's love.

His children were raised with this message of God's love in the front of their minds and one child began to follow in Alex's ministerial footsteps. Edgar attended Bible college and upon graduation, he felt the same strong call to use creativity to preach the Gospel—just as his father had before him. Alex never pushed Edgar into occupational ministry because he

has been reaching an all time high in Winnipeg. In 2016 it was reported by CBC News that this non-native species infested a police station in Winnipeg. We can only speculate it all started at the Okay Repair Shop?

10 In Alex's journal he wrote during this time - *"In my leather and shoe shop on St. Mary's Ave, outside of my shop I had a sign with a large broken heart painted on it and it had a crack right through it. The words on it were "We fix anything but broken hearts." This morning a young lady walked into my store and she had been drinking and was very talkative and she mentioned my sign on the front of the shop and said, "I sure wish I knew who could repair my broken heart!" Well this gave me an opening so I told her – I can't fix broken hearts but I know one who can and so this being a Saturday I invited her to our church about three blocks away – The Calvary Temple in Winnipeg – for the morning service and then she could hear about the expert on broken hearts. The following week we found out that this lady had been to the church and was wonderfully saved and she had mentioned about how she was at my shop on Saturday. We were not at the church that day but out of the city for some reason. So we praised God for using our sign of a broken heart."*

knew firsthand it was not an easy life, so when Edgar accepted ministry as his lifetime calling, Alex knew it was from God's influence.

Alex was a loving father and had always been a clown at heart. He was adored by all children and was always sharing jokes and magic tricks. Because of this, Alex's name was modified by loved ones and he was gifted the moniker "Smart Alec." Amazingly, it was Martin Clausen (the former street kid from Denmark that had been rescued from a life of homelessness through Marie's boarding house, and who had voyaged across the world in pursuit of marrying Marie's daughter) who taught Alex the magic technique of "sleight of hand." Nobody knows exactly where Martin had picked up this skill from, but perhaps it was something he had used in the streets to beg his bread. Years later (and on the other side of the Atlantic Ocean) Martin married Laura Rasmussen and transformed from a street kid into a jewelry shop manager, and even went on to open his own store in Calgary, Alberta, called *Martin Jewellery*.

After a 2,293km move to Vancouver, Alex began to further explore culture and art for inspiration in how to creatively share a message. In the late 1940's Alex became drawn to the use of puppets and really hoped using them would prove to be an engaging tool to share God's message of hope.

Dating back thousands of years, puppets had been a mainstay in storytelling, and in the mid-1900s, they had a resurgence into the mainstream across North American pop culture due to television. It was increasingly common to see puppets in entertainment as they began to make appearances on *The Howdy Doody Show*, and in the acts of Jimmy Nelson and Edgar Bergen (featuring puppets: Charlie McCarthy & Mortimer Snerd). These acts in the first half of the century paved the way to the 1955 birth of Kermit the Frog, arguably the world's most famous puppet. In order to sell something in the 1950's "post-war era," the message did not have to be packaged as sexy to appeal to customers. Entertainers and advertisers found that using puppets was a humorous and lucrative sales tool for all ages.

Alex developed a charming production inspired by three things: his own love for children, the magic skills taught by Martin, and the discovery that magic and puppets combined was a genius way to captivate an audience. He built an 8x6 foot puppet stage and fabricated functioning puppets from dolls he purchased. His production proved to be captivating and effective in communicating the message of Jesus. This revolutionary production incorporated music, ventriloquism, magic, and hand puppets. It was geared towards youth, but he was pleased because it appealed to all types of people. His unusual act sparked curiosity and drew a non-churchgoing crowd into the church where they were treated to unique entertainment and the story of God's plan for redemption. This was done through engaging with the creative ideas found in popular culture of that era, trailblazing ministry methods, and not compromising the message of the Gospel.

Initially Alex and Fern performed the puppet shows as a duo. Later their children, Edgar and Eunice, joined them and they traveled together sharing the gospel throughout British Columbia. They dubbed themselves *A Family Crusade*. Eventually Edgar and Eunice started their own band and called it *The Rassmussen Musical Party*. When Edgar became newly married, and as this new style of family-music group evangelism became in high demand in the late 1950's, he and his wife Marilyn began to branch out and do some of their own travelling shows while their young family grew and grew. They eventually came to be known as *The Rassmussen Singers*.[11]

Unbeknownst to the Rassmussens, they were part of a

11 Alex's wife, Lavina Mae Fern Rasmussen nee Morrison (1904-1968), passed away on December 12, 1968 and is buried in Burnaby, British Columbia, Canada. Alex re-married to Millicent (nickname Millie) in 1969. She was also very good with puppets. Together they traveled with their puppet show and then became youth pastors at a Chinese church in Calgary, Alberta. Alex passed away on March 18,1983 in Calgary, Alberta at the age of 84 and is buried at Queens Park Cemetery (Lot; 36, Block; 35, Section; N). Millicent passed away on May 4, 2007 and is buried with her husband. Alex lived to witness the birth of his first great grandson, Philip Shorey, the fourth generation since their voyage from Denmark.

dawning of itinerate ministers across North America who were also using magic, ventriloquism, and puppets. It soon grew into a full-fledged movement as more preachers began to explore the performance arts to communicate their appealing message. There was a wind of the Holy Spirit that breathed over the continent, and it inspired many free thinkers and evangelists to present the same message of Jesus Christ in fun ways never before imagined at that time. It was humorous, colorful, and a breath of fresh air that challenged the stale traditions of that day.

Creative gospel communication became a large part of evangelical culture during the mid-to-late 1900's and appeared in many different art forms. In 1953, the *Fellowship of Christian Magicians* was formed in California, with magicians like Dr. Joe Kemp and André Kole.[e] There were also the hippie musicians of the Jesus Movement, *The Jesus Film* in the 1970's, and the traveling evangelistic family-acts that continue to this day.

It seemed that early Christian magicians were helping to pave the way for magic to become an accessible form of entertainment. By the 1980's, secular magicians such as David Copperfield brought magic further into the public's interest when he famously made the Statue of Liberty disappear and walked through the Great Wall of China. Mainstream audiences were demanding more magic and many of the traveling Gospel acts were already established and ready to meet the increasing demand for this kind of entertainment! Even more Christian families joined the movement and drew people into churches through their shows that travelled throughout the United States.

Alex was not known (or previously documented) as a forerunner of this creative movement, but considering his timing in the use of artistic ministry starting in the late 1940's, he was certainly an innovator of evangelistic performance arts. What he did pushed the envelope of traditional Christian evangelism and opened the door for relevant artistic communication. Although his legacy has not been previously chronicled in Christian publications, there is no doubt that his creativity and passion for Christ helped to ignite a generational calling that continues to this day.

Generation 1 is based on Marilyn Rasmussen's photo albums and holiday stories, Kelvin Ketchum's research, Edgar Rasmussen's memory, Aksel Rasmussen's journal, the ancestry research of Brenda Lukinuk, and the Give Museum in Denmark - Give Lokalhistorisk Arkiv.

SWAN RIVER COFFIN

TOLD BY AKSEL (I.E. ALEX) RASMUSSEN

———————•◆•———————

(1922)

SOME YEARS AGO while stationed at this Salvation Army Corps, my lieutenant was just out of Bible school from Winnipeg – his name was John Sullivan. He was older than me and well advanced in Bible knowledge. He had seen previous service in the army and even though I as the commanding officer was so much younger than he, he never went ahead of me or took advantage of me. We enjoyed working together, and each took our turn at the cleaning, washing, and cooking as well as platform preaching. One early morning, I noticed that the lieutenant did not sleep so sound, and when time came to get up he said, "Captain, I've been in prayer nearly all night and I feel God wants us to do something out of the ordinary to get people to our meetings. He asked me to let him preach Sunday night instead of the morning, which was his turn. I said, "sure lieutenant." Then he said, "I want to go to the undertaker and borrow a coffin for Saturday night open air to preach from as well as Sunday night at the church." Well, I was a little afraid of the idea, as Saturday was always our biggest attendance on the street corner at anytime.

The main street was only about a long block away, and almost all the business stores were in that block. We had already been asked by some of the storekeepers if we would move the open-air meeting into the park across the street. I felt it could start real trouble to do this on Saturday night, as the complaint was that the people stood listening to our open-air meetings and left their shopping to the last hour or less, and this made it very inconvenient. We settled by having the coffin for the Sunday evening service only.

We went to the undertaker and he let us pick the one we wanted. It was a very large one to be able for us to stand up inside. Needless to say, the hall was full before the 8 o'clock service and even some of the other church people were there. After the song service and prayer, Lieutenant got up and made a few remarks before he got into the coffin. He gave his testimony that he was all ready to meet God and if he did not finish his message and should God call him home that the people listening should "just leave my body here. I'll be better off." He entered the coffin and read this scripture from Job.

"I know that my redeemer lives, and that in the end he will stand on the earth. And after my skin has been destroyed, yet in my flesh I will see God;" - JOB 19:25,26

He began to preach and in just a little over half an hour there was a great moving of the Holy Spirit—some were in tears, and others came forward to the altar as we sang an invitation chorus. There were a number and we did not have enough helpers to speak to them all.

After the service we managed to speak to most of them. Among the seekers was Mrs. Elliot, the sheriff's wife of Swan River. The following day we were busy visiting and praying with most of those who came forward. We gave all the Glory to God. Praise His name.

PHOTOS

Philip Shorey's family by Johannas' blacksmith
home in Give, Denmark

Johannes Rasmussen

Marie Rasmussen

The Rasmussen kids before they traveled to Canada

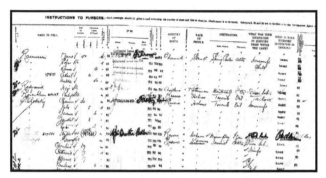

Ship log from the S.S. Laurentic

Alex in The Salvation Army

Alex Rasmussen

The Rasmussen family outside the Okay Repair Shop

Cow horn souvenirs Alex made during the Great
Depression

Alex and Fern traveling with Edgar and Marilyn

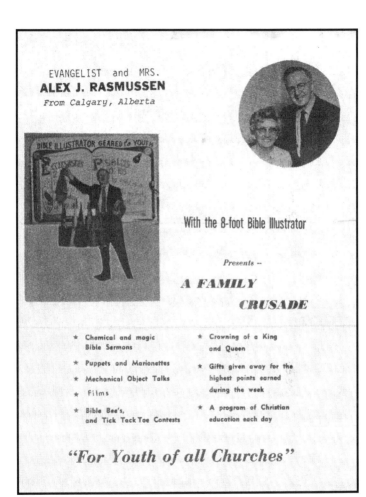

A flyer from their show

Alex and Fern's Bible marionette theater

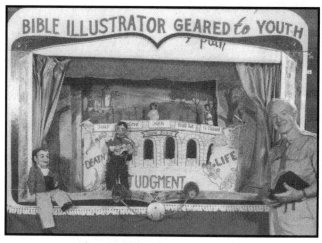

Alex and his marionette show

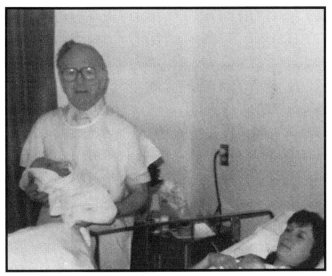

Alex holds Philip Shorey

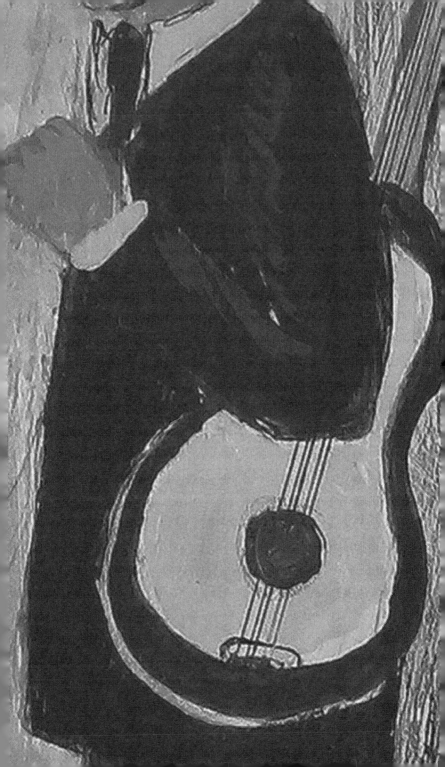

GENERATION 2

⇉⇉⇉❬❬❬❬

FOLLOWING THE RASMUSSEN'S struggles to stay afloat during The Great Depression by shining shoes and living behind their storefront, another widespread tragic event struck: World War 2 started on September 1, 1939. Calvary Temple in Winnipeg began to host late night prayer vigils, which were attended by many people. Some travelled great distances to be there. There was a looming fear during these years and the war drove many to truly seek God with a desperate heart because human systems were failing and weren't worth trusting. Many men and women attending the prayer services at Calvary Temple made the decision to follow Jesus. This was the church that Alex and his family were attending.

At the age of seven, Alex's son Edgar attended one of these late night prayer vigils. He was seated in the first row of the balcony because the church was packed with people. Edgar heard the pastor preaching on the subject of heaven and hell and when the pastor asked for those who wanted to receive Jesus into their hearts to raise their hands, Edgar stretched his hand skyward. A deacon saw him perched in the balcony, and asked Edgar if he could escort him down to the altar for prayer. Edgar joyfully agreed. From that point on Edgar said, "YES" to Jesus and wanted to be a preacher and a pastor and enthusiastically shared his commitment to this decision with everyone he met!

At that time in Winnipeg, the snowdrifts would get as tall as the telephone lines and people walked to church and school in -40F weather. In the winter of 1945, Edgar developed double pneumonia when he was 12 years old. Edgar was very ill and on the brink of death when one night around 3am, Edgar heard his name being called. He looked at the foot of his bed and saw Jesus standing there with his arms wide open and saying, "I love you." Edgar knew that if he was allowed to live through this illness he would gladly carry this message from Jesus Christ everywhere God would permit.

The Holy Spirit did come through for Edgar's health during this bout of illness, but the doctors strongly advised his family that they needed to move him to a warmer climate because of his weakened state of health—or he would most certainly die before the age of 18. Following such a serious warning, the family relocated in 1946 to Vancouver, British Columbia, on the west coast of Canada. Edgar was scared, and uncertain of his future, but knew God was with him and had a plan for his life.

In the years that followed, modern medicine and health struggles remained testing-grounds for the faith of some Rasmussens.[12] As an adult Edgar has never forgotten how real and how faithful Jesus had been to him throughout the difficulty and uncertainty of his health. He felt called to creatively preach the Gospel after graduating from *Lighthouse of International Foursquare Evangelism Bible College* (L.I.F.E.) in 1952. All his worldly possessions fit into his new Chevy, including an acoustic guitar and an accordion. He loaded everything up and began touring Canada—from Vancouver to Toronto. Over the next two years, he visited every Foursquare Church in Canada—recruiting students for his alma mater and preaching the Gospel. He felt compelled to visit little towns and country churches on the outskirts of modern development in order to share the message of Jesus in a way that would shake things up a bit.

After those early days of travel a ministry group began to form, and included Edgar Rasmussen, his sister Eunice, and his friends Wallace & Donna Stelting and Carl Osterberg. Together,

---

12 In 1948 God healed Edgar's mother Fern, of a mental illness. She had been in a government institution for a year when she called Alex and shared that she heard something snap in her brain and that Jesus had healed her. Alex came to assess her because he knew if he took her home he would lose government funding for her institutionalization which was very risky if she wasn't really healed. After further assessment, he determined that she was truly healed and brought her home. When Edgar was 17 he came down with an unusual medical condition. The doctors didn't know what it was until after he had suffered with it for 50 years. In 1982 Dystonia Torticollis was discovered and Edgar was eventually diagnosed and treated for it.[f]

these five like-minded and enthusiastic individuals made up a little band which later grew to become a more elaborate band that included a mandolin, three accordions, two guitars, a violin, and of course, a musical Singing Saw![13]

Over time, his evangelistic modern band consisted of many different members and formations, but Edgar and Eunice solely kept it going no matter who joined their *Rasmussen Musical Party*—that was until one day, while he was speaking at a camp and saw a mysterious woman that caught his eye.

Her name was Marilyn White and she was the camp pianist. Marilyn had received classical piano training at the Toronto Conservatory of Music. In addition to her being a talented pianist, she also aspired to be a world-class figure skater—but following a sacred and powerful encounter with Jesus, she sold her skates to buy a Bible.

Marilyn was in some ways larger than life in her aspirations and her faith, and her prayer life was no exception. She was born with asthma that affected her in every way, but during a healing meeting lead by William Branham in Vancouver, she was prayed for and believed to be healed. She told everyone she was healed only to have a week of the worst asthma attacks of her life starting a couple days later. Well, unbeknownst to the skeptics, during that week she coughed up a bowls worth of black mucus and never had issues with asthma ever again!

Edgar knew when he saw Marilyn that she was the one for him; she however, had determined to never marry a preacher. Her hopes were set on traveling the world and she sought to do this as a stewardess. Her desires to see the world was being further cultivated by her hobby of communicating with several

13 When Edgar was a teenager his father gave him carpentry saw for Christmas and encouraged him to play music on it. The instrument was reminiscent of Alex's Scandinavian roots. That Christmas was around the time the post-war musical Singing Saw revolution began. Prior to World War 2 the Singing Saw had become a popular instrument for church, Appalachian folk, and Vaudeville Theater but as a result of the war, steel became very expensive. Much of the knowledge of the instrument died in the war because saw players were predominantly male. After the war, when the cost of steel came down, the instrument had a revival.[g]

foreign pen pals. But God must have had other plans. Edgar and Marilyn were married on November 16, 1956, and in God's loving character, her heart's desire to travel was accomplished through becoming the wife of a traveling evangelist!

For about six months, they traveled and performed throughout British Columbia as a *Family Crusade* with Edgar's parents, Alex and Fern. They lodged in homes of local church members and had two shows daily. This was before families had their own televisions, and people were hungry for entertainment! The townspeople would come out to a Billy Graham styled "crusade" and would be treated to an enthralling variety of marionette shows, musical performances, and storytelling. Entire families would make the decision to follow the Lord during these shows and be welcomed into a relationship with the local church community.

Edgar and Marilyn continued to travel for two to three years at a time while performing, preaching, and relying on God every step of the way as their family began to grow. Word got around of their traveling family act and the demand for them to broadly tour in the United States was petitioned by the Assemblies of God. In 1963, Edgar and Marilyn travelled south with their three children who had been born during their time in Canada. Then during their time on the road they had two more children, Kyle and Philip[14]—who were born in the United States.

Edgar had built a 9x11 foot puppet stage that they packed into a thirty-four foot trailer which they towed behind their car as they crossed into the United States. Their props included thirteen marionettes (purchased from Hazelle's Inc., a Kansas City puppet company), German hand bells, an accordion, and the Singing Saw.

On and off for nine years, they traveled in their camper trailer

---

14 Today the members of *The Rasmussen Singers* have all together twelve kids who are all serving Jesus (Philip, Tyler, Lacy, John-Mark, Bryce, Kramer, Kayla, Kaitlyn, Brielle, Blake, Shelly, and Jared). Edgar and Marilyn also revered Patricia Ullman as a daughter and she has two children named Sarah and Justin.

through windy roads and winter storms. As they performed throughout the United States and Canada, they shared with many people the message of Jesus and intermittently pastored a couple of churches—eventually landing them to pastor Reedsport Assembly of God for twelve years in Oregon. They finally put down roots, building and pastoring Glad Tidings Assembly of God (Now called Inspiration Bible Church) in Tacoma, Washington for almost 30 years.

Marilyn cultivated in her kids a love for Jesus at the altar and a love for music at the piano. Although their musical outlets have varied, all of Edgar and Marilyn's children have carried on the legacy of keeping Jesus the focus of their musical art forms and lives.[15]

In the 1960s (at the peak of vocal harmony pop groups), Edgar and Marilyn established their musical act as *The Rasmussen Family Singers* and released an LP on vinyl. This era of traveling evangelistic family bands was the musical predecessor to "Christian Rock n' Roll" in the 1970s, even though drums in church and "Christian Rock Music" would face a steep resistance from the previous generation. The creative marionette movement also continued to thrive and draw crowds up until the cultural swing of the 1970s when Dick Myers and Jim Henson brought hand-rod and human-arm puppetry to the mainstream through television and film.

Generation 2 is based on recollections from Edgar Rasmussen and documents written by Marilyn Rasmussen.

15 On December 9, 2013 Marilyn passed away after a long fight with cancer. Her ashes are placed in the Resurrection Wall of Life Center in, Tacoma, Washington. The moments before she passed, she told her husband that she had just been walking around with Jesus and was going home. She lived a very fulfilling life as a pastor's wife, massage therapist, and piano teacher. Her passion revolved around God and her family. On August 7, 2016 Edgar remarried to Patti Lanning Ingle, whom they had met in Reedsport, Oregon.

MODERN MIRACLES IN THE LIFE OF A YOUNG EVANGELIST

TOLD BY MARILYN RASMUSSEN

————◆————

(1959)

I WAS A new mom with two small children. We had recently purchased an old trailer with one axle that was far too heavy to be pulling with our green 1956 Chevy station wagon. Edgar purchased that station wagon when it was brand new, just before we were married. He had to take off from preaching and fell trees as a logger for several months to afford it, and we loved the privacy it gave to our little family as we traveled in *A Family Crusade* across the country. Fresh out of Bible school, my husband travelled all across Canada for two years representing his former Bible college and then travelled with his sister and friends. After marrying him I had my first experience to travel, and up until now, traveling in evangelistic work held a sense of romance and adventure and each crusade was so fulfilling and gratifying as older folks, and kids as well, responded to our Bible marionette puppet stories and illustrated Gospel messages.

The first part of our itinerary for this trip had been in the Okanagan Valley in British Columbia and now we were headed to a two-week crusade scheduled in Kimberly, B.C. On our way to Kimberly, we would have a short stop at a camp in Kootenay, B.C. in the midst of the beautiful coastal range. Desiring to help an elderly lady on a pension, we picked her up from her church in Osoyoos, B.C. and were planning to take her as far as Kimberly where she would catch a train to complete her journey to Regina, Saskatoon.

We travelled south in the Okanogan Valley and crossed into Washington to avoid the steep ascents; however, the pull from Tonasket, Washington, eastward caused our car to repeatedly boil over. Fortunately, there was a stream below where we could fill our containers for our thirsty car.

Once we arrived at Republic, Washington, we made a decision to continue on towards Kettle Falls. State workmen were laying frost pipes on the mountain road so when our trailer and car tried to drive through these areas we got bogged down deeply into the sand. Someone came up with the idea to push the trailer from behind and it was attempted (we later discovered this attempt caused all of the connectors in the pigtail to break), but the workmen instead opted to pull us through six more frost pipe areas all the way to the summit.

It was perfect driving down from the pass (for about three miles) and then all of a sudden one of the trailer tires blew! In taking off the flat tire my husband's watch was smashed. Then he had to go to Kettle Falls, about a forty-five mile distance, to purchase another trailer tire. When he returned with the new tire, our jack would not lift the trailer high enough to mount a fully aired-up tire. In a matter of minutes the Lord provided all the help we could need as the workmen (who had previously pulled us through the frost pipe areas) were now heading home and they immediately recognized us. They had jacks galore to help put on a trailer tire. We rejoiced to once again be on our way.

Soon it was dusk and we needed trailer lights. This is when we found out all the wires were broken in the pigtail, and my husband, in the dark, tried for hours to repair the car and trailer connections. Finally he fastened the six wires from the car to the six wires from the trailer.

It was getting late into the night when we finally crossed back into Canada and onto Rossland, B.C. five miles farther, and 2,000 feet lower, is the town of Trail. The road is very twisty and the descent is very steep. Because the trailer was so heavy, the station wagon was unable to hold it back and we began to pick up momentum. Faster and faster down the winding road we went. Ed's hands were gripping the steering wheel and every turn became a frenzy. Each family member desperately calling out to the Lord for protection when all at once a large area with lots of boulders appeared. The car bounded over the rocks banging the oil pan and Ed threw the car into park and stopped at a large turnout area. The brakes were red hot—on both the car and the trailer—and we sighed a great sigh of praise to the Lord. After what seemed like hours, the brakes had time to cool down and we proceeded much slower and cautiously down the rest of the winding hill into the sleeping little town of Trail. It was the wee hours of the morning when we gassed our station wagon at the only service station open in town, which was a Shell Station.

The hill out of town was long and straight and steep with the Columbia River on one side and a mountain on the other. Our load was too heavy and a valve burned out allowing us to ascend no faster than three or four miles per hour. Again we desperately called out to the Lord in fervent prayer and inch-by-inch, little by little, we reached the top. The Lord had heard our prayer and we rejoiced, but even on the level our car still would not accelerate more than 15 mph.

The next towns were Salmo, and then Nelson, and our day's destination (Kootenay Pentecostal Camp) was only an hour away. In Salmo we were just passing the last street light when all at once another trailer tire blew and a U bolt dug down deeply into the asphalt, fastening the trailer to the middle of the road. The car did not have enough power to pull us loose. Our elderly passenger decided that perhaps we were accustomed to "evangelistic travel" but she was not, and inquired if we would please take her to Nelson where she could stay with a friend and then continue her journey by train to Regina, Saskatoon—she had more confidence in the train to get her there safely. Ed stayed in the trailer with our children, Brad and Shawnette, and I drove our friend in our crippled station wagon to Nelson with my foot to the floor, but travelling no more than 15 mph. There's a long winding hill down to Nelson, and there was hardly a car on the streets. We finally found the address of my passenger's friend but no one answered the door—so she decided to go to a hotel instead. A Royal Canadian Mounted Police noticed our late wanderings and stopped us to enquire. He gave us directions to a hotel and cautioned us that an inmate had escaped from a local institution and had already killed a lady in a farmhouse back at Salmo, so everyone had been warned to not open their doors.[h]

After delivering my passenger to the hotel, I had the long, winding hill to ascend. The station wagon would only go at a 'snail's pace.' I was at the end of my rope. I had had enough for one day. This evangelistic travel was not what I expected. I fussed at God. I was not a happy evangelist's wife. I was angry. The more I spewed, the slower the car moved. Would it quit altogether on this God-forsaken, deserted road?

I was alone...God was my only refuge. I began to call out to Him. "I will lift up mine eyes unto the hills, from whence cometh my help. My help cometh from the Lord which made heaven and earth." I fervently called out to the Lord to intercede to fix the car. There were many more hills to climb, and it was slow climbing. I became repentant and broken, and Jesus heard my cry —and the car began to accelerate. Faster and faster until it was doing almost 60 mph by the time I was at the top. My faith now was big enough to move mountains, even the Cascade Mountains. Now I became convinced that even the trailer tire would be fixed and we'd be on our way, but disappointment overcame me as my headlights reflected on our aluminum trailer that was still sitting lopsided in the middle of the road. I pulled up behind the trailer and sobbed bitterly. My husband wondered why I didn't come into the trailer and approached my window to find me slumped over the steering wheel. In an instant he drew my attention to the nearby tire shop and in a few hours we were on our way to camp again.

We had a good first day at the camp and our baby daughter Shawnette was dedicated to the Lord by the guest speaker Rev. Claire Scratch. His father had dedicated me when I was a baby twenty-three years earlier. Our plans were to stay at camp through the weekend and to help provide some of the music; however, Ed felt impressed to call the pastors at Kimberly where we were to start our next crusade. Perhaps they would prefer us to come a couple of days earlier. The pastor's wife, Florence Bell, answered the phone. Her husband was up north hiking through forests and fording rivers to Kitimat. Kitimat was a company town planned and built by the Aluminum Company of Canada in the 1950s, and the pastor was going there to pioneer a new church. Florence Bell didn't have anyone to preach on Sunday, and she gratefully accepted our offer.

We returned to the road, and as we approached the Balfour ferry dock a new challenge awaited us. The provincial toll ferry was the only means of connecting the highway, and in those days there was a toll for vehicle and driver—additional tolls for every rider and even more because of our trailer. We had spent most of our money replacing trailer tires and could only come up with a couple of dollars in piggy bank money. I inferred that we could not continue this way but Ed asked what the alternatives were. There were none. We were going on that ferry. As we approached the dock we could see that no one was there to accept fares. We drove aboard the ferry just following the line of cars and still no one came by to take any money. Thirty-five minutes later, we debarked and our ride was absolutely free. We were dumbfounded. In utter amazement we drove on, without further incident, all the way to Kimberly. The pastor's wife welcomed us with open arms and we inquisitively mentioned our free ferry trip across the Kootenay Lake. A young man entered into the conversation and explained that this Saturday, August 1ˢᵗ, 1959 was a special celebration in British Columbia. It was Burning of the Bonds Day and to celebrate the toll may have been removed.[16] God again had guided us and had provided miraculously.

Many years later, in the summer of 1990, we were asked to

---

16 The toll was charged daily until October 1963 when tolls were removed from all bridges in British Columbia and the Kootenay Lake ferry.[i]

be the camp speakers at the boys and girls Kootenay Pentecostal Camp. So once again, we travelled the same road reminiscing our first trip with the trailer thirty-one years prior. It was surprising to observe that there was no large turnout area on the narrow winding road down from Rossland to Trail where Ed previously had to throw on the brakes and parked. As we shared our travelogue from decades earlier to camp staff members (that were also local residents), they also insisted that there's never been an all-night Shell Service Station in Trail.

God is still the God of modern day miracles to this day, and because He lives, we too shall live. This has been one of the experiences that has helped us in our faith walk in our many years of ministry. Jesus never fails and we never walk alone.

ANGELS IN THE NIGHT

TOLD BY MARILYN RASMUSSEN

———— ◆ ————

(1960)

IT WAS JANUARY 6, 1960, and Edgar and I, along with our two children Brad (26 months) and Shawnette (8 months) started out early this wintery morning to drive from Vancouver, British Columbia, to Melville, Saskatoon. We were in our 1956 Chevy Station Wagon, which was fully loaded with children's ministry equipment. We were going to pick up our trailer, which we had left in Melville, Saskatchewan that previous November, and then travel south to Iowa where we had a full schedule of "*A Family Crusade.*"

After we held hands in prayer, my father slipped us a $20 bill as we said good-bye. We also had a Shell credit card to take us to our destination, but that was all the money we had.

The day went well as we drove the Hope-Princeton highway in B.C and we enjoyed the wintry beauty of the mountains and snow laden alpine trees. Hour after hour, we drove very cautiously as we had no chains and some parts of the highway were covered with black ice; however, most was hard packed snow.

Our immediate destination was to reach the US border crossing, just south of Grand Forks, before it closed at midnight. In doing so, we would avoid the dreaded Cascade Mountain passes between Grand Forks and Rossland, BC.

You cannot imagine our utmost dismay and disappointment when we saw a barricade across the road at the border control preventing anyone from entering the United States. We had missed the customs patrol by only fifteen minutes. With only a few dollars left, and unable to stay in a motel for the night, we had only one choice and that was to drive the three dreaded Cascade Mountain passes.

It was a gorgeous night. It was so bright from the moon and the trees weighed heavy with new fallen snow. We were now breaking a fresh trail on a new snowfall. We turned off the car lights to see if we could drive without them and we could still see perfectly. The mountain scene was so beautiful. Ed drove carefully and cautiously on through the night.

We rejoiced as we crossed the first pass and again a while later as we passed over the second. It was now the wee hours of the morning, we had not seen a single car, and we were still breaking the trail when all at once Ed lost control of the car and it veered to the right and off the road into the snow-filled ditch onto its side. Ed pushed his door upward and crawled out and up onto the road. The load shifted inside. The children and I were leaning heavily onto the opposite door and the children were upset with the new position they found themselves in. Ed stood on the road scratching his head as he surveyed one very hopeless situation.

We still had not seen a single car all night and now what in the world were we going to do? We had no familiarity with where we were, where we might get help or how we would keep warm on the mountain in the car if Ed had to walk for miles to get help.

Ed stood in a quandary of thoughts when suddenly headlights appeared. An older couple drove up and out jumped four young, tall, slender men. One of them wore a cream-colored lightweight jacket and a second fella wore a pale blue jacket and third young man wore a tan jacket. I don't recall the color of the fourth. None of them had on hats and their hair was of light brown color. They stood on the road with Ed viewing our station wagon on its side in the snow-filled ditch.

We asked, "Whatever are you guys doing out here on a mountain pass this hour of the night in these summer jackets?" and their reply was something to the effect they were driving around looking for excitement and adventure. But then they added, "It looks like you really buried yourself in the snow. No problem. We'll have you out in no time."

Four young men got down in the ditch, one at each corner of the car and in less time than it would take you to read the remainder of this story, we were sitting upright on the road all ready to continue on our way.

Ed stood in awe and thanked them for their help. They wished us well and then jumped into their car and continued on their way in the direction we had come from. Ed and I looked at each other speechless and in utter amazement. It had happened all so quickly we were dumbfounded. Who were these men? Where had they come from?

We drove silently in thought on the trail broken by our rescuers, and as we rounded another mountain bend we realized there were no longer any tire tracks ahead of us. Could these men have been angels in the night that God had assigned to minister to us in our need?

PHOTOS

Edgar and Eunice

Edgar in the streets

Edgar and his band

Marilyn and Polly the parrot

Edgar Rasmussen

April 1956

That dashing evangelist, Edgar Rasmussen

Edgar and Marilyn get married

Edgar and Marilyn

53

Edgar plays the Singing Saw

The marionettes getting some publicity

The marionette stage

Those German hand bells

Traveling with the family

Edgar, Marilyn, Shawnette, and Brad

The Rasmussens

The Rasmussen Family Singers

Giving an altar call

Family Crusade flyer

The family band

The Rasmussen Singers album

GENERATION 3

>>>><<<<

SHAWNETTE WAS THE second oldest child of Edgar and Marilyn Rasmussen.[17] She was born April 3, 1959 in Vancouver, British Columbia, where her parents built a home base near Marilyn's father, Leslie White. The family spent three more years using that home base while performing their show—mostly around British Columbia. Then they crammed into a motorhome and headed down to the United States.

After nine years of being on and off the road, while rearing five children, plus juggling between marionette performances and a few pastoral jobs—Edgar and Marilyn recognized they needed to find a new way to fulfill God's calling in their lives. Space was getting very cramped in their camper with five kids.

Reedsport Assembly of God Church in Reedsport, Oregon, had grown a deep fondness for the heart of this creative family ministry. They were impressed by their vision and the show's effectiveness. It was also God's timing for the family to indefinitely move out of the tight camper walls and into a new life. The Reedsport church hired Edgar to be their pastor. Town life suited the family and they enjoyed their time there—with the exception of the encounters Shawnette had with local bullies.

When Shawnette was a young girl, she was often teased for her small skinny frame. This teasing caused her to become quite shy, but despite the bullying she was determined to minister alongside her family and found her own special gift in singing. Shawnette became a very talented singer with a strong solo vibrato. During the family's ministry on the road she became very creative and developed a deep foundation for art, the Lord, and a love for her family.

Shawnette's creativity expanded into fashion after she

---

17 Brad and Craig were born in Canada. Kyle and Phil were born in the United States.

received some very nice clothes from her mother and rejected them rudely. In response, her mother bluntly declared, "From this moment on, you will make all your own clothes." Marilyn remained true to her word, and Shawnette had to learn how to design and sew her own clothing from that moment on.

Around age 13, many life-altering events occurred for Shawnette. One event was when a young evangelist named Bob Swope visited her family's church as a guest speaker. He was a gifted ventriloquist with a puppet named Charlie. As a young boy, Bob was also very bashful, similar to Shawnette. So, his mother bought him a ventriloquist puppet to help him "break the ice". The puppet opened up a world of ministry opportunities for him. He was an amazing artist and Shawnette was enthralled by his stories.

Through Bob Swope's Gospel message and Shawnette's weekly meetings with a church-based scouting program, called Missionettes, she said, "YES" to God's heart for children. She was beginning to understand that God was calling her to tell the next generation about the love of Jesus—even despite being shy and insecure. Her mother bought her a book called *Ventriloquism in a Nutshell* to spur Shawnette's confidence and creativity.

Then heartbreak came for Shawnette when Polly, her beloved pet parrot, passed away. She mourned the loss, but at the same time this event was powerfully changing Shawnette. She set her mind on creating a parrot puppet; however, this is not a morbid Frankenstein tale of a heart-broken child trying to bring her old friend back to life; rather, this was the dawning of a new era for Shawnette! This was a story of a determined and hopeful young woman who used her talents, skills and interests to create something completely new. Her ability to sew (which she begrudgingly acquired after rejecting clothing purchased by her mother) became a blessing in disguise. Shawnette could now design and fabricate more than just clothing—she could make her own puppet.

Shawnette didn't plan for her parrot to become a

ventriloquism figure, but after a week of locking herself in her bedroom to fabricate Polly the Parrot, and zealously reading the ventriloquism book her mother had given her, the family was beginning to get a little nervous by all the strange noises they heard coming from her room. By the end of the week, she emerged a full-fledged ventriloquist!

The next thing Shawnette did was completely outside of her bashful character. She signed up for the local school talent show with Polly the Parrot. Together, they stole the show and completely brought the house down by making fun of all the teachers. She began to perform with Polly around town, at churches, and community events. She even performed for a few week-long "Kid's Crusades" in neighboring Oregon towns with her mom. Eventually she saved enough money and bought her first wooden ventriloquist dummy and named him *Arney*.

People couldn't figure her out. For most of the day Shawnette was a quiet, reserved, and petite person, but when she placed a puppet on her hand and had a stage under her feet, she opened up like a butterfly with a jet engine flying out of a stinky cocoon! She began to realize who she really was! Pushing aside the scrutiny she felt from others, Shawnette channeled those jokes into stage humor and chose to tune into the calling God had placed on her life.

The next big step for Shawnette was to enroll in Bible college. In 1977, Shawnette left home for Northwest Bible College in Washington State with the hopes of becoming an educated Children's Evangelist, but she discovered that there weren't any classes on children's ministry at that time. Children's ministry in church was not yet deeply established, so there were no mentors to teach her. She had to seek out other ways to continue her own creative education. She was among the first of many creative-minded Children's Pastors.

Years later, her younger brother Phil was on staff at Northwest Bible College, and called upon his sister for feedback and expertise in children's ministry. Shawnette became an adjunct professor for the subjects of puppet operating, designing, and performing for kids' ministry. She taught the very subjects that she wished she could have taken while in school.

While still attending Northwest Bible College, Shawnette met her future husband. Later they would lovingly joke together about the time she was waiting in line at the cafeteria for lunch with turkey on the menu, only to meet John Shorey.

John Shorey had been raised in Maine but had come to the Northwest by way of Alaska where he was living his dream as a true "last frontier" marksman. He had just received Jesus into his life while working in the logging camps and was discovering God's love in his life like never before. Now, having made Jesus his first love, as opposed to his passion for competitive shooting, this East Coast woodsman was at Bible college seeking God's calling on his life which, unbeknownst to him, included falling for this young, pretty woman who had a passion for children's ministry!

Shawnette wanted nothing more than to do Children's Ministry, but as a child she had visited Alaska and her memories of this "last frontier" had made a positive impression on her. While there, she panned enough gold to purchase her first 10-speed bicycle. Perhaps John tried to woo Shawnette with the following words, "Marry me and we can live on an island in Alaska, where the wildlife is beautiful and the mountains are breathtaking—but most importantly, there are lots of Inuit children who need to hear about Jesus!"

John and Shawnette were swiftly married in December of 1978 and then they moved to Gravina Island in Ketchikan, Alaska. John was building a home there and it did not have running water or electricity, until he contracted a helicopter to carry a windmill to his property, which made it the first to have electricity on the island. The newlyweds pioneered a new life together on the island and served together in Ketchican at a local church as children's pastors. John also worked part-time at a hardware store and quit being a logger because the life expectancy of a logger was very short. He wouldn't want his kids to grow up without a dad.

Shawnette would get flown out to remote Inuit villages on a floatplane to perform ventriloquism. She carried the message of Jesus in creative ways into places that not many others could visit. The children in the villages were skeptical and reserved towards outsiders, but they loved Arney, the ventriloquism dummy. Together, puppet and evangelist would attract entire villages due to Arney's insulting antics and his humorous romantic behavior towards the pretty native girls. Shawnette bridged the understanding of Christ's sacrifice by contrasting Arney's flawed love to God's perfect love for all people. Many people in the villages came to appreciate this timeless message.

Those years in Alaska include many moments when the couple recognized God's goodness. Once they were certain that a huge wave would capsize their little motorboat as they commuted across the straight to downtown Ketchikan. They were miraculously spared from that wave, but became inspired by the story of Moses floating on a basket in the Nile and from then on transported their first-born son, Philip, in a buoyant cooler chest so he would miraculously float if necessary.

While reminiscing over the seven long years living on an island in the wild, Shawnette recalled that for her, one of the best things about Alaska, was what came *out* of Alaska; gold, memories, and the Shorey family. God was doing something special, but the couple felt that a piece of the puzzle was still missing from the overall picture of what God wanted to do with their lives. Prayerfully they felt led to embark on the road with a traveling show to present the Gospel for family audiences across America, much like Shawnette had done growing up with her family.

Before starting their full-time travel, God brought Shawnette and John to Tacoma, Washington with their two little boys, Philip and John-Mark. It was there that they set up a home base with their family and prepared a traveling production while

Philip started taking piano lessons.

Philip didn't want to take piano lessons, but his grandmother, Marilyn Rasmussen, was a gifted pianist and a clever woman. One day, he heard one of her other students performing *Ode to Joy* by Johannes Sebastian Bach. Afterwards he asked his grandmother if she would teach him to play *Ode to Joy* as well. She agreed, but only after some scales. As soon as he had tried it once he said, "Okay, that's enough for me," and tried to slip away. She grabbed him by the arm and said, "Oh no you don't, now you will learn to play the piano." She tricked Philip into learning piano and continued to direct his musical education by sometimes forcing him to practice his songs twenty times perfect (in a row) before he could eat his supper, which his mother had to rescue him from on occasion. She also made it fun and fostered in Philip the same love of music that she also bestowed to her own children.

Grandma Lyn (Marilyn's nick-name from her grandchildren) had a long history of family travel; however, she knew she would miss the Shoreys so much. She understood the temporary sacrifices sometimes required of people in ministry, but whenever she spoke of her daughter's family she would bemoan that they would be gone forever. She was pained when the day drew closer for them to leave because her life revolved around her family and God.

One way she made sure to keep them coming back was she bought Philip a little American Eskimo puppy. That way he would always look forward to seeing his dog when he would return back to Washington. They named him Nikky, or "Nikky–Wild Dog of the North" from the Disney movie, because he reminded Philip of Alaska. Nikky was fierce, fast, and a miracle dog. He definitely had an impact on building the faith of the family.

One day, just before Philip and the family returned for Christmas, Nikky had jumped off a high porch and hung himself by his collar. Grandma Lyn came home and pulled up on the driveway, only to see right in front of her: Nikky, swaying back and forth, completely limp. She quickly grabbed him and started to do mouth to mouth CPR on him; crying out to Jesus, "Please bring Nikky back! Philip will be here in just a few days and he wants to see his dog. I can't tell him his dog is dead. Please bring him back!!!" And what would you know, that dog came back. This happened three times! Not always by way of hanging. Sometime by way of getting hit by a car, but lo and behold, Grandma Lyn did CPR, prayed in Jesus name, and the dog would come back to life every time; talk about a lasting impression on the power of prayer and care for God's little creatures. It was a sad, sad day when Nikky passed on from old age.

After about a year of preproduction, the show was ready and the Shoreys had no intention of ever settling back into a typical home life. *The Shorey Family's Lighthouse Ministry* hit the road with rod-arm and live-hand puppets (culturally relevant in the 1980s Jim Henson Muppet era), magic, singing, clowns, ventriloquism, and a pirate rat costume for Philip (who firmly refused to participate in any clown related activities). It was a complete family circus! Shawnette was taking what she had been given (a family, a loving heart, and creative skills), and pulled it all together with her innovative and hardworking husband who envisioned how to materialize and fund her passion. The family set off for an unforeseeable future of great risk, at an extraordinary cost, but with a life of high purpose to reach families for Christ. They found a fulfillment that a normal life could never bring.

Word of this kid's crusade got around and they traveled to many places across the continental United States. The family was also given a couple of opportunities to return to Alaska for ministry. They toured many Inuit villages and small towns with their show. Here they could reach out to kids and families who lived off the grid, in small shacks and with planks for pathways over their muddy trails. For a week at a time the family would camp in a village, perform a show every night, and then set off again for another village. They were being God's hands and feet and He was drawing entire families into the local church. The altars were filled with families accepting Jesus into their lives and weeping before the Lord every night. As the Shoreys traveled between destinations they were constantly graced by God's beautiful gifts of nature—magnificent northern lights and the sights of little bear cubs wrestling on the side of the road.

Initially, Philip and John-Mark loved the road. They saw almost every state before third grade and gained a widened worldview and incomparable education by the "school of life." They saw God provide when gasoline was needed or food was scarce. They learned how to serve God in creative and simple ways, and after each show Philip was actively involved in praying with people as they entered into the family of Christ.

Having the children on the road required a lot of energy and planning, but their presence was a joy and their role in the body of Christ was invaluable. On one occasion the family was doing a ten-minute commercial on a Sunday morning service in front of nearly 1,000 people. John-Mark was a toddler, and situated above the puppet stage and instructed to swing a rubber lobster on a rod. The local pastor was seated next to the puppet stage and trying to maintain a respectable "pastoral" appearance—but then John-Mark attacked the pastor with a rubber lobster and completely stole the show. The congregation was roaring.

After several seasons of touring, the family became road-weary, and it became evident to John and Shawnette that their kids needed a static home that would be more conducive for making friends. There had been a church in Derry, New Hampshire, that had seen enormous fruit come from the Shoreys' visits, so they offered John and Shawnette the position of children's pastors in 1990 at the height of the children's church puppet ministry movement.

New Hampshire was a sure fit and the family called it home for ten years so the kids could grow up. Philip graduated high school from Pinkerton Academy. Then, Philip headed to Minneapolis, and the other three members of the family moved back to Washington to continue in children's ministry there.[18]

Working with children was very rewarding for them. Shawnette can remember many people who have told her, "I came to Jesus as a child because of your performance." Others have shared with her that even though they walked away from faith as a teen, they came back because of the foundation laid in their youth, while attending their crusade.

"Reaching children leaves behind a legacy of fruit for generations to come that one may never know about." – Shawnette Shorey

The rise of the "children's church puppet team" was a phenomenon that undoubtedly made an impact on the American churched youth of the 1980s and 1990s in creativity and understanding of the Bible. The movement was in large part fueled by *One Way Street, Puppet Productions,* and *The Fellowship of Christian Magicians.* Secular society still adored puppetry, which increased the cultural relevance of the church. Children's ministry curriculum included popular characters on *Gerbert* and *The Gospel Bill Show* while puppetry in mainstream cinema continued to flourish through films like *The Muppets, Star Wars, The Dark Crystal, Gremlins, The Neverending Story,* and *Labyrinth,* along with puppet driven television productions like *ALF, Mr. Rogers, Lamb Chops, Fraggle Rock*, and *Sesame Street.*

In 1995 Pixar released *Toy Story*, and ushered in a new era of computer animation in child friendly films that would, by the early 2000s, do away with almost all puppetry in pop culture entertainment. This, in combination with the rise of the internet in the late 1990s, seemed to open the door to more screen led education in children's ministry.as well as public schools. Eventually computer technology and cartoon animation became the standard for children's education and entertainment. Puppetry became less desirable for practical and

---

18 The story of John and Shawnette Shorey continues as they live in Arizona and work as a voice for end-times theology.

economic reasons, which eventually made it also less culturally relevant for the church. It appeared that within American culture puppetry would now take a different path—ride the coat tails of nostalgia or go back to the underground from whence it came.

Generation 3 is based on the memory of Philip, John, and Shawnette Shorey.

COAST TO COAST

TOLD BY JOHN SHOREY

———◆———

(1986 - 1995)

OUR FAMILY OF four traveled for five seasonal stretches in the late 1980s. The first year we did kid's crusades in my home territories of Alaska and New England. After our first year, we had made enough contacts in the United States that we could fill a whole tour season on either coast. We very seldom had an available week that didn't get filled, and we were booked close to forty-five weeks each year.

We never made any demands for a certain cost to bring our show. It was our heart's desire to reach kids and parents for Christ, no matter the size of the church. Through this we quickly discovered that the church size was not related to the generosity.

Once, when we were in great need of financial provision, we were grateful to be scheduled to perform at one of the largest churches in northern Maine. We arrived on a Friday afternoon and were about to set up for a weeklong crusade, but upon our arrival we were informed that they had sent us a letter of cancelation two months prior. This had never happened before and we had to make a quick decision. Do we try to fill this canceled week with only one day to do it, or do we go down to my Aunt Leota's camp on the lake, to avoid spending money, and enjoy some fishing and jelly beans? The kids really did love

Aunt Leota and her passion for sharing jelly beans with them at that lake.

Then I remembered that a month before we had connected with the pastor from a small church in Ellsworth, Maine. He was originally from Oregon and he had known my wife's family. We hit it off really well and he expressed his desire that we would come and do a kid's crusade at his church. Our tour was booked solid, but I agreed to call him if we had a cancelation.

Well, now we had a cancelation—and it was time to give Pastor Burt a call. When I called him, he confided that this short notice would leave them no time to promote and their funds were low. They could not make any financial commitment to meet our needs. I told him that we were willing to come in faith and that God would meet our needs either during or after the crusade. God had led us to have faith for our needs with a threefold strategy:

1)   A donation based honorarium by the church.

2)   A food list for people in the church to sign up and bring us meals and food items.

3)   An exciting way to take kid offerings. (We would fill two ten-gallon aquariums and place a large plastic tug boat on top of each. One was labeled Boys and the other Girls. Then the kids would bring all their change for their offering to fill the other gender's boat. We would lower the boats into the two aquariums at the same time and the winner would be the gender that sank the other boat first. This competition would reward the winning side with an extra scoop of ice cream on the last day of the crusade. We kept our ministry afloat by sinking boats!)

Most of the church attendees in Ellsworth, Maine, did not hear about our coming until Sunday morning during the announcements— when we did a ten-minute preview with our stage set up and a puppet skit with the full details that would excite the kids for the coming week.

Despite knowing they had very little finances to support us, Pastor Burt chose to take a special offering that Sunday morning. There was a doctor who was vacationing in Maine and God moved on his heart to place a generous offering toward our ministry. It turned out that the financial support from this small church was larger than what we had previously received from one of the largest churches in the district. It reinforced the lesson that we must place our confidence in God and not on the outward appearance of a church.

Pastor Burt Lowry later reported that "kids' ministry became very critical to us over time, and two of my daughters went to Valley Forge Christian College and got degrees in children's ministry," while his son Jon, who was no doubt inspired by the music and ministry of these touring ministries as a kid, went on to join a renowned worship band called Unspoken.

The greatest blessings have been seeing the fruit of our ministry. We always promoted our crusades to be family crusades and would often see parents dedicating their lives to Christ along with the kids. Once we visited a church in Washington with a great-sized building that held only a moderate size congregation, but when we came they almost packed the whole church the whole week of the crusade. This church had done a lot of prep work. They had canvased the whole community to bring out a crowd. A year later, I heard the report that during our crusades they had doubled the attendance of the church and their numbers had not diminished.

One time we went to a church in Elmira, New York, that had 300 kids in their children's church, and by the end of the week they had 900 kids attending the crusades. We had about 50–75 people coming up front to receive the Lord every night—kids and adults. In fact, it was very common to see adults.

Some of our most memorable crusades were to the native villages in Alaska including Klukwan and Minto. We visited these locations twice during our years on the road. The turnout in these villages was almost the total population of the community and Shawnette's ventriloquism dummy Arney, was always the hit of each evening meeting.

Shawnette would always open her ventriloquist routine by knocking on his trunk and asking him if he was awake. "Arney, are you awake?" Then she would throw her voice in the trunk so it sounded like he was talking to her and telling her to go away because he was sleeping. Then she would tell him that there are lots of pretty girls out here. This always seemed to motivate Arney to get ready to perform. He had many acts, even one wearing a muscle suit and pretending to be Hulk Hogan the world famous wrestler.

Upon our return to Minto, Alaska, (two years after our initial visit) we were walking through the village the day before the crusade would begin. As we walked past a couple of cool young teens, they initially ignored us. Then they turned around and shouted, "Did Arney come back?" Of course he had, and when they had learned that, they came out for the whole crusade.

Back on the East Coast we were on our way to do a crusade in Saugas, Massachusetts. It was a really hot day and we traveled with a super cab F-250 Ford pickup and pulled a thirty-seven foot fifth-wheel trailer. Our engine was overheating, but I pushed on to get to the church. We made it—but blew the head gasket on our engine, and the real damage happened the next day. Water had leaked into the cylinders, and when I went to start the truck, I blew the engine. We needed to have the engine rebuilt and it would take almost three weeks; however, in less than a week, we were scheduled to arrive in Derry, New Hampshire for our next kid's crusade.

The church in Saugas didn't have extra funds to help us. They didn't even have the money to buy the copy machine they desperately needed, but the pastor of the church was Ron Turner, and he just happened to be the former pastor of our next church in Derry. He knew all the families in Derry, and knew that Dean Burman had a fifth-wheel trailer with a strong truck to pull it. Pastor Ron called Dean who drove down to

Saugas and hitched us up and transported our family and trailer to Derry.

We had a great kid's crusade in Derry, and loved our time there with Pastor Richard Stevens, but at the end of that week we had another crusade to get to right away. Our truck was still in the shop, so Dean delivered us to our next crusade in Riverside, Massachusetts, and then, a week later, back to Saugas, to collect our repaired vehicle.

Back in Saugas, I felt the Lord telling me to buy them an $800 copy machine—even though we had a $2,000 truck repair bill and only six more weeks of crusades before the Thanksgiving and Christmas season—when we were unlikely to receive any income.

Miraculously, over the next six weeks we covered the truck repairs, all our travel expenses during the crusades, our return trip to Washington State, and had enough surplus to cover all of our living expenses during the downtime over the Holidays.

Two years later, we were back on the east coast and doing our second crusade in Derry, New Hampshire. Pastor Richard Stevens told me that if we ever got tired of traveling, we should consider coming on staff as Children's Pastors in Derry. A year later we took them up on that offer. My sons needed a stable place to grow up, so we adapted our calling and served there for five years.

We settled there in the early 1990s, when Jim Henson-styled Muppets were rampant in children's ministry across the USA. Companies like *One Way Street* and *Puppet Productions* provided us with baseline curriculum and, since Shawnette came from a legacy of puppetry, she always added her own twist. We converted a horse trailer into a puppet stage that performed in local parades and did Singing Christmas Cards in the local malls. We started a local puppet team and called our group *The Power Puppet Team* (A pun on *The Power Team*: a popular body building ministry of that time). The people who became puppeteers and involved in the group steadily grew.

Many families became lifelong friends to us and were creatively inspired like Darren Rockwell – The Magician. Many more families came to Christ through the ministries of the *Power Puppet Team* from a small church in the small town of Derry, New Hampshire.

PHOTOS

Shawnette and Polly the Parrot

John Shorey as a logger

Arney the ventriloquist puppet

John Shorey

John and Shawnette get married

Kid's Crusades

Philip and John-Mark living in a camper

Philip helps his Dad on stage

Performing in Minto, Alaska

Shawnette preaching in Alaska

John and Shawnette Shorey

Shawnette with Arney as "Hulk Hogan"

Philip, the only non-clown member of the family

Kid's ministry in Derry, NH

The horse trailer puppet stage

GENERATION 4

$\Rightarrow\!\!\!\Rightarrow\!\!\!\Rightarrow\!\!\!\Rightarrow\!\!\!\langle\!\!\langle\!\!\langle\!\!\langle$

IT WAS IN those early years of traveling in a camper with my family; after leaving the orcas that would swim past our home and walking on the beach with my dad collecting washed up toys in Alaska—that I (Philip Shorey, the eldest son of John and Shawnette and first grandson of Edgar and Marilyn) found Jesus. Time and time again Jesus delivered us from roadside problems and provided for us with all we needed. The provision we experienced made a huge impression on me as an innocent little kid. I grew to trust my Heavenly Father. I was able to watch his angels lead the way and bring life, hope, and change to people everywhere we went.

I loved praying with kids my age after each performance, as they would come up to accept Jesus at the altar. I loved exploring new places and dark halls of church buildings when nobody was around. I loved counting the coins with my dad that were given in the offering game; and seeing how those small individual gifts added up to be enough for gas money. We always tried to find the wheat pennies for my collection. All in all, I loved experiencing God in authentic ways *and* playing with all the toys in each church nursery.

There was one night I had an unforgettable encounter during my time living in Tacoma, Washington. We were staying with my grandparents, Edgar and Marilyn, and preparing our family show to get ready for the road. I was trying to fall asleep when I heard footsteps enter into my bedroom, but there was no one there. I grew completely afraid and then recalled I had been taught, "Nothing can stand up against the name of Jesus." I didn't know what else to do, so I just called out to Jesus and said, "In Jesus' name, GO AWAY." In response to my command I heard the footsteps walk away. Shortly after that, the footsteps returned and I repeated the command again. This happened three times, and after that third time the footsteps completely stopped. I fell asleep after recognizing I had been told the truth and that spiritual battles occur—but with Jesus' help I can be safe when I sleep. I told no one about this at the time, because I assumed nobody would believe a little kid.

Another time, when we were on the road, I remember praying with my mom and brother before bed in the camper. I felt the Holy Spirit fill our traveling home so strongly I was brought to tears. I didn't know what was happening, and my mom asked me, "Why are you crying?" I simply replied, "Because I love Jesus so much." It was an amazing experience to feel the love of God so strong in our camper at such a young age.

Some people might say I was young, brainwashed, and impressionable, but I know otherwise. God revealed Himself to me in a way that I could understand at my age, and it's still in His character to reveal himself to people of all ages in ways they can understand. It doesn't matter if a person is young or old. I felt his presence, it was real, and it changed my life.

In 1990, my family moved to New Hampshire and stopped traveling to become children's pastors at a church in Derry. Road life was becoming too difficult and I had struggled to make friends, because I had lived as a traveler from such a young age. It was hard to relate to others. I was very shy, as my mother Shawnette had been, and was also teased for being skinny. Being in one place for a week, trying to make friends, only to say good-bye a few days later really became tiring for me. Thankfully my parents recognized this and God provided the next step for us.

When I entered school in New Hampshire I found that I was naturally athletic and soccer became my resource for making friends. Puppetry became less and less important to me while soccer became more and more a part of my identity. In fact, because of soccer, I started to feel cool. Meanwhile, puppetry was losing its cool factor pretty quickly.

Once, after becoming so enraged for losing a soccer game, I realized the sport was becoming an idol and was controlling me. I went into the woods behind my house and cried out to Jesus to show me who I was to Him instead of all this. I needed friends, and sports were the means for this, but I didn't want it at the cost of my God and my temper.

On that day I gave up my plans to play soccer and chose to follow God's plan for my life. I said, "YES" to Jesus and started forming my identity around who I am in Christ, and nothing else. I vowed never to touch a soccer ball again unless God wanted me to. In hindsight I can see a generational parallel between this experience and my Grandma Lyn's ice skates for a Bible exchange, and my dad's marksman to a minister surrender. I now held my dreams with an open hand, took my faith into my adult life, and applied it to life decisions. I fell in love with the Bible and started to read it with such a freshness that it was as if it had been glued shut and I had never seen it before. I couldn't get enough of it.

Shortly thereafter, while reading the Bible before bed, I looked over to the window and I saw a shadow with two red eyes duck down as if it didn't want to be seen. This was terribly odd considering my room was on the second floor and I wasn't allowed to watch horror films, so I had very little Hollywood influence over my imagination. At that moment, a shudder went through my spine and I felt a dark and intruding presence flood into my bedroom. This perverted and evil presence was lingering there, so with the lights on, I buried my head in my Bible and began to cry out to Jesus. I refused to look around to see what was there. I did this for a few minutes until the dark sensation went away and I felt an overwhelming peace enter the room in its place. I had found Jesus again in a new stage of life and it wasn't theoretical. It was a real, victorious, and strong love.

Soon after that, when my faith and identity was being made new, I was faced with a new crossroads. Was I to find new Christian friends or remain faithful to the punk rock friends

I had made? I struggled with this because I really wanted more Christian friends, but I couldn't find any who were willing to participate in the weird music things I loved doing, and I couldn't stop caring about my punk friends from school. Who was going to be a light to them and show them who Jesus was, when they were so wrapped up in getting wasted and going to shows?

I talked to God about what friends I should have, and I stayed true to my punk rock friends. I was given a new love for them and for music. I tried to not be super impressed with the cultural scene we were part of and I wanted to follow Christ in a way that was different than living in a Christian bubble that I saw encouraged in the church. Many of the punk rockers I knew had grown up in church like me, but were starting to hate Christians because of the hypocrisy they observed in the lives of their parents. In contrast, I had already had, and was having, real encounters with Jesus.

As an angsty teenager, Christians were getting on my nerves as well, but I couldn't deny Christ had worked in my life and was still working in me. I could not exchange the mark that Christ put on my heart at such a young age for popularity with my peers. I would play in bands with these friends and drive them home after house shows when they were drunk and puking. When they died, I mourned, and when they were mocked by jocks, I listened. To the best of my ability I shared my faith when I could, I gave reasons to believe in a loving God and challenged their atheistic beliefs when walking to class together. It didn't matter if they were labeled Satanists, punks, goths, or Marilyn Manson freaks, I only felt God's love for them.

When the Colorado Columbine shooting happened in 1999, I sympathized with my friends, who were receiving flack for wearing long trench coats—similar to the ones the shooters had worn. I listened to their deep pains as they were ostracized and disparaged. My local church and family did not understand my love for the punk scene and I felt like they labeled me a "black sheep" for choosing to hang out in the "wrong places" and for going to see bands with "terrible sinful names" like, The Trailer Sluts and Toxic Narcotic. My mom would cry at my bedroom door asking God to save me, and so I began detaching from my family.

Unfortunately, so many of my family and former friends misunderstood me as well. During a Christmas visit my grandmother marched into the basement to yell at me for listening to "Satan's music" and give me a hard time for having messy hair. It seemed to me she would lovingly, but misguidedly, buy me proper trendy clothes as Christmas and birthday gifts to conform me to her preferences, rather than accept me for who I was.

This dogmatic and image-based belief system wasn't what I found in the radical God I had met on the road as a young child; this was something else I was learning to identify as Christian legalism and religion. It was a disheartening and subtle tactic the devil used to sneak into Christian communities—and not even my family with their fruit-filled Christian heritage was immune to it.

Despite their doubts in my integrity, my family's love did not waver for me and I knew God had a plan for me, my talents, and growing passions. He had brought me to hurting people that didn't know any other Christians and couldn't relate to the church's corporate whitewashed walls. They needed to hear it from one of their own. I was unaware at the time, but the loving prayers of my parents and grandparents probably kept me safe in some sticky situations, even though they didn't fully understand my heart or agree with my method.

In 2000, I moved to Minneapolis. I attended North Central University with piano and music as my major, partly because I wanted to be in the Midwest where culture was passing from coast to coast, and partly because I knew that after a number of years in the punk scene I needed a break. Without much mentoring, and being alone in the mission, I knew too much of the punk scene was becoming part of my identity just as soccer had. I wasn't going to make that mistake again.

My three-semester stint at North Central abruptly ended because I acquired a repetitive use injury in both my wrists and the pain made extended piano practicing unbearable. I had to quit playing piano for a while in order to heal. I had to move off campus and I wasn't sure what to do next or if I should even stay in Minneapolis. I made a cold call from the yellow pages (which was still a thing in 2001) to a commercial recording studio and landed a film music internship in Northeast Minneapolis at the Northrup King Building. I decided to stick around and pursue a film career instead of hopping a train.

One evening, after getting settled into my new apartment and internship, I visited a Christian community at a home called the Steiger House[19] for their Monday night community meal. I had heard about the house before through a variety of unexpected characters including a rock star from the band Five Iron Frenzy and a crusty train hopper. The communal concept of this place intrigued me. Maybe it would be similar to the church in the book of Acts. My heart had been asking, what is church? What did the church in Acts really look like? Was Acts real? I wanted to be part of that if it was! It seemed radical and relevant to everyday people. I liked that.

At the Steiger House I encountered an old acquaintance named Benjo who was now the leader of a local group called The Scallywags Bike Club.[20] I vividly remember sitting and eating dinner with The Scallywags and hearing Benjo share about a circus concept he was considering.

The idea was that the circus would tour around the nation and be designed to bring people to Jesus. I thought, "Hmmm... I've done that before!" In fact, I recently had a desire to do it

---

19 Steiger International is a worldwide mission organization that is called to reach and disciple the Global Youth Culture for Jesus.

20 The Scallywags Bike Club was a Christian Bike Club that rode freak bikes called Tall Bikes and aimed to show love and be a light to anarchists through creativly showing people Jesus.

again—and that surprised me because it had been much for my sake that my family had stopped traveling. I had just wanted to live a normal life like all the other kids I met and go to a normal school. But now that I was grown-up and had experienced the normal life, I hoped God had something more extraordinary for me. Now I even felt an urge to travel and I knew it came from Jesus because I thought I was done with that.

It was surprising to find myself amidst a group of likeminded people who were working to create a ministry similar to the family traveling act I had grown up in; however, this time it was a spooky bizarre show and they needed creepy circus music for a "Christ-centered extravaganza."

My classical piano training and recently discovered interest in classic horror had nurtured in me an innate ability to compose creepy circus music—which I frequently did late at night under candlelight like a phantom of the opera. It didn't matter if I was in a dingy old basement or a secluded country home. I became inspired by the environments and imaginings of harlequins jumping to and fro while I pounded out new monster music to my delight. During this time I had also fallen in love with the music of world-class composers like Philip Glass, Bernard Herrmann, Max Steiner, Danny Elfman, and the Kronos Quartet. The opportunity to use this strange talent for Jesus was fantastic! I desired to do something for the Lord, but I had never considered that creepy circus music could ever be used for Jesus. I didn't know how it could fit into ministry because people who attend church typically don't worship to creepy circus music.

In 2002, I began to compose the music and write the show with a panel of others who also had a calling for the show. Together this beast of an adventure was undertaken. Those were some crazy days and I learned many lessons that I won't ever forget. After many grueling months of preparation The Scally-Waggin Circus presented *"Madness of Folly:"* a gypsy* styled circus musical!

In 2003, the Scallywags purchased a homemade circus

wagon, which opened into a stage and the show toured during the summers of 2003 and 2004. We premiered our show in Bushnell, Illinois at Cornerstone Music Festival, and then toured across the country to California with the bands Headnoise and The American Culture Experiments. It was truly astounding! We were an eclectic caravan of 30 people attempting something incredibly groundbreaking. It felt like many years were added onto our lives because of the variety of experience and the richness of the challenges.

Despite all the hard work and stress, our mission was clear; we were to bring the Gospel to people in a wild way *outside* the walls of a church. This was a total paradigm shift from the conventional evangelistic methods that had been the standard practice in America and in my family for generations. But this was a new era and a revival of the early Salvation Army values, which brought the spiritual conversation to the public square and into the street; greatly inspired by the creativity of William Booth's marching band.

There had been a cultural shift since the previous generation. Baggage from unfortunate church experiences, lack of relevance, and the onslaught of entertainment had made it difficult to use the church building as an evangelistic tool. We just *had* to go to people. This pursuit would stick with me and become my individual creative calling—well beyond my time with the Scallywags.[21]

Other creative projects also began to take root during these early years in Minneapolis. I began working as a composer for a local underground theater and got to see many types of puppet productions trickle through using paper-mâché, marionettes, and shadow puppets. The puppets and the performances made me reminiscent of my childhood, but were abundantly different. Instead of a message about Jesus, these puppets aggressively promoted eastern religion, politics, anti-family values, and beer.

---

21 To learn more about *The Madness of Folly*, and the lessons I learned during its pre-production and tour, read the chapter *Art as an Idol* in the book *Kill Your Art.*

I already had given up puppets in high school because it seemed very childish and I wanted desperately to fit in and be cool. But before that time I loved puppets. I even participated in puppetry competitions at the Fellowship of Christian Magicians conferences and won national awards year after year in the 1980s.

Now my eyes were being opened to how influential the art of puppetry really was and I started to realize that it wasn't always just a foam tool for impressing little kids. Puppetry performance was for anarchists and artists too. It was avant-garde and intellectual work. Although the content didn't always sit right with me, I knew I was working in that theater for a reason. It was not a coincidence that I moved to Minneapolis from New Hampshire and found creative and spiritual hubs that were a perfect fit for me and unlike anything I could have ever imagined or pursued on my own.

I was in the center of a creative underground movement and working on what I loved; meanwhile, I found my heart was breaking for the people around me, just as it had in New Hampshire with the punk rockers—and this time I fell in love with those I worked with in the theatre scene. I still held fast to my convictions as they presented spiritual alternatives and philosophies intent on bringing down a manmade government only to replace it with another hopeless and breakable manmade system. They had radical hearts to restore the health of the earth; while at the same time they destroyed their own bodies with drugs and alcohol. I saw their attempts at selfless love for each other through sex and human aid, contrasting their hate for their yuppie corporate neighbors and the demonization of people who opposed their cause or tribe. I wanted to help them see the truth.

I knew that a purposeful and fulfilling life worth living would not be found in these things. True life meant loving one's enemies, taking care of *all* creation, and not heeding to any manmade system as the hope for the future. True life meant following the Creator of it all, who was the ultimate example of selfless love, and was more like a loving father then a tyrannical dictator. I wanted to be less known as a culturally "Christian" American (and all the modern baggage accompanying that title), and more recognized as an advocate for healing the human heart through the name of Jesus. I wanted to achieve this with art as my vehicle and the Holy Spirit as my guide.

I would ride my bike to theater rehearsals and it became my prayer closet on the way. Sometimes tears would flow out of a broken heart for my coworkers. I would have to stop and pull off the road to wipe my eyes so I could see again. God was very close to me, and I had been given an incredible privilege to spread His love in this underground place which was unknown to most Christians and where I thought no Christians would ever go. [22]

I was continuing to write music for other people's stories and having my story/testimony be my life. I had not considered developing a show myself until I meet a very famous puppet maker.

People kept saying I needed to meet him and that my music with his puppets would be wonderful. Then I met him at a party and he invited me to his studio to discuss possibly working together on a production. I felt very honored and I knew this meeting would be special.

As we sat down and began to talk, I was very open with my faith because that's just how I am. He didn't seem to mind and in fact he seemed very intrigued. As the conversation evolved he told me about something he had done in Mexico with a little puppet show he called "The 45." They were 45-second puppet shows housed in a shoebox and used for busking on the street.

---

22 I would actually learn that after my time deep in the underground theater scene, there had been other believers who had been called to build puppets and work in close proximity with the same people years after I stepped away. As I grow I have learned that God sees the big picture. He has an even bigger broken heart for people and is over time sending multiple urban indigenous missionaries to be His light to the world. He cares just as much about his disciples as those he wants to reach, which is why He can use us, and then take us out for a time so we don't get goofy.

I loved to busk and would sometimes play the accordion and the melodica on the street for grocery money- before I found out about dumpster diving (then I used the money I made to pay rent).

When the puppet maker told me about these shows, I had an epiphany moment as my random passions collided and lined up in perfect symmetry. BOOM, it all made sense! Why couldn't I build a stage similar to what he was describing and design mine to cater more to a slightly larger audience?

In response to me verbally processing my revelation, he mentioned something similar that had been done by a priest that he knew and respected. The priest would dress up like a clown to travel, and perform the sacraments out of a suitcase. As we talked further it began to all make sense to me; music, marionettes, busking, theater, travel, and Jesus. Then I brainstormed with him something that I had heard from Benjo (the leader of the Scallywags) about life in the slums of Brazil.

While Benjo was on tour in Brazil with the band *No Longer Music*,[23] God had made it very clear to him that he needed to go back with a servant-team to care for the poor on the streets and bring hope to the glue sniffers, prostitutes, and drug dealers.

The team had great ideas about welding rickshaws together and helping in other humanitarian ways, but in recent years God had given me a heart for kids through my job as a piano teacher. So what about them? What could we do to reach out to all the generations in the slums, young and old? How could we really love the outcasts and not just put a bandage on the situation by helping for a moment, but provide the truth and hope for the heart and soul that could carry on long after we would leave? This would be made even more challenging because it needed to be achieved across a language barrier. A marionette show could be the answer! A marionette show could carry a message

---

23 *No Longer Music* is an evangelistic rock opera that started in Amsterdam in the 1980s. It is lead by David Pierce who is the founder of Steiger International. Read the book *Rock Priest* to learn more.

like that in any language.

Henceforth, I was determined to develop a puppet show that would fit inside a suitcase or, better yet, a treasure chest. I settled on a steamer trunk, like something used for voyaging on the *Titanic*. It would need to adhere to the growing number of restrictions about size, technology and materials allowed while flying. This growing list was being enforced by a new government agency, called TSA, which had been formed in response to the September 11th, 2001 terrorist attacks. This would be tricky because the performances would be on the streets so the trunk/stage would need to be built with self-contained lighting and sound.

Naming this globe traveling wonderment would have to be descriptive and true to what it was. I certainly needed to steer away from the mid-century influence of calling every evangelistic effort a "crusade" (that might have worked back then but today it carries a lot of unnecessary and irrelevant baggage). After a long bike ride, I thought of something with a bit of a tongue-twist to it. It was "The Suitcase Sideshow;" *Suitcase* because it travels—*Sideshow* because Jesus was the main event and I'm just happy to be on the side, doing my part while watching the greatest three-ring circus (Father, Son and Holy Spirit) change lives forever![24]

The inclusion of the word *sideshow* was also a beautiful metaphor about our openness to any of the people to whom we might present our show before: even to outcasts, those in the streets and in forgotten places. All were welcome at the sideshow. All could find a new life, acceptance, and love at the sideshow. "There you can find, seated around the same table playing cards together, a woman who weighs six hundred pounds, a girl with a

---

24 The name Suitcase Sideshow also came with the dream that it would be a sideshow to the Scally-Waggin Circus, but when the circus ended, The Suitcase Sideshow carried on the original mission. Another influence to the name came from the film, *Freaks* (1932) by Tod Browning.[k] This was a film about sideshow performers who were ridiculed and mistreated but found an oasis in the circus. In a way, The Suitcase Sideshow was for outcasts, as a place for them to find love and acceptance from God, just like the original sideshows of the golden age circus.

body shaped like a frog's, and a man with three legs. The person shuffling and dealing has no hands, he does it all with his toes." "Nobody sits around feeling sorry for himself or anybody else... You can be accepted there if you had nine arms and ten heads."[j]

Thus, my quest to build a traveling marionette street theater began—and everything was falling into place. Gifted writers, painters, engineers, and electricians all surfaced in my community and wanted to help out. A local improv group called *Happy Fun Time* provided assistance in script writing and supplying voice actors. Through them I met Wes Haula, a gifted scriptwriter, and Mark Anderson, a gifted engineer and inventor.

Marky turned out to be a total genius. Anytime I imagined a strange contraption, he created it. After my housemate and I constructed a 12-volt lighting system from motorcycle parts, Marky helped develop the sound system from a motorcycle amp, and later updated the lighting rig to use modern LED's (that weighed significantly less than my original design) and 9-volt powered motors.

There were many things Marky and I did to keep the show lightweight and compact, but there were many other inventions we dreamed of but knew they hadn't even been developed yet for such a compact design. Through the years there was an increasing consumer demand for portable technology and minimalistic design. This made our ideas for using triggers and automation—blending an old-fashioned style with new technology, computers, and strings—more possible. I felt like James Bond empowered by Q; Marky was a talented inventor doing his part in this unique mission to save the lost on the fringes of society all over the world.

I was absolutely in awe of the talent that was being shared to produce and fabricate my show; a true testament of the Body of Christ working together for a common goal. With hunger for God working in my life, I began to fast and pray 2-3 days a week. I rode my bike with tears running down my cheeks as I felt the Holy Spirit encouraging me that I was on the right path, and the lyrics of a hymn became my anthem: "The cross before me, the world behind me – no turning back, no turning back." Aside from that truth written so decisively in the hymn "I Have Decided to Follow Jesus," I didn't know what was ahead of me and I didn't feel prepared, but I was desperate for God to use me and equip me because I knew that alone in my own strength, I would never be ready. I knew that the God I serve used Moses for conversations despite his speech impediment and equipped David in battle, despite his size. I leaned into the notion that God doesn't just call the equipped, He equips those He calls.

It took over a year to build the stage and lights, write a script and music, record and edit all the voices, and find people willing to assist me, but I knew this calling was from God—and I knew no matter how hard or how long it would take, I had to do it. God had put everything that I loved together in one box for me to pursue and give back to Him: theater, travel, music, busking, recording, performing, and most of all, telling people about Jesus.

Finally, all I needed was marionettes, and not just any marionettes, but ones made at the proper size and weight. I recalled that my grandparents had traveled for nine years with marionettes and I wondered where those marionettes were now. I called my Grandpa Edgar to inquire. He said they were collecting dust in the basement and I could use them with "no strings attached." Astonishingly, but not surprisingly, after I stringed them up, they were the perfect size and style that I needed.

Then it hit me—I was repeating family history for the fourth time! All of my adult life I felt as if I was the black sheep of the family, and now I was learning I was exactly like my family, and for the first time in a long time, I truly felt proud of it. As these thoughts surfaced, God also breathed into me a fresh love for my family, and I began to heal.

I grew in my understanding of how much God loved me, and

saw that the prayers I had said for years, pleading that He would heal my relationship with my parents, were being answered through a show that wasn't just a ministry to others, but also a ministry to me. I realized that God had even bigger plans for me than I could have imagined on my own—and if God can change my life, He could change other people's lives as well, and that is worth making art about. It is worth letting others know the loving and life changing character of Jesus and that they can also start a generational blessing for their children's children by taking the step of surrendering their lives to Jesus, and asking the powerful question, *"What is it that you want me to do?"*

"You shall not bow down to them or worship them; for I, the Lord your God, am a jealous God, punishing the children for the sin of the parents to the third and fourth generation of those who hate me, but showing love to a thousand generations of those who love me and keep my commandments." - DEUTERONOMY 5:9,10

So here I was, with much of my daily activity being consumed by puppets... again. Not again in a negative way, but this time in a way that said, "YES... I'm not imitating my family's tradition or just along for the ride; I'm imitating a calling from God, and for that I feel blessed to have been seen by the Creator and chosen for a great work."

As this show was being developed, I asked myself, "If I could make one show, and communicate one thing to the people of Brazil, what would it be?" Over much fasting and prayer, it came to me. I would say, "No one has gone too far from God's love that He can't give them another chance at a life worth living." With that, I decided my first show would be "The Story of Saul's Conversion."

Before I could ever feel right about taking my performance to Brazil (and invading as a green outsider who really had no concept of the cost involved in what I am doing), I needed to take my show and risk it all in Minneapolis. What place would be better to debut my new theater then the very place that reintroduced me to puppetry. I began to prepare for a show at *The Bedlam*, the biggest underground anarchist punk theater in Minneapolis.

Generation 4 is based on the memories and journaling of Philip Shorey.

THE FORBIDDEN PUPPET SHOW

TOLD BY PHILIP SHOREY

———————— ◆ ————————

(2005 & 2020)

THE PREMIER PERFORMANCE of The Suitcase Sideshow was for my neighbors, family, and friends at the Christian community house where I lived. The house was called the Oakland Hotel and my studio was in its dank and dingy basement. The feedback from the eight guys who also lived there had been paramount in my verbal processing of creepy marionette ideas.

The stage was set-up in the garage and the garage door made a perfect curtain for the crowd positioned in the alley. My Grandma Lyn and Grandpa Edgar Rasmussen were, by a miraculous coincidence, visiting me from Washington State and present in the audience. After my performance, they shared stories of how God had used the exact same marionettes fifty years ago through their ministry around the continent. Many neighbors and friends came to witness the heritage of this new show and be a part of sending it out into the world. To me it felt like a "passing of the baton" experience that grounded me and reminded me that this wasn't about me, or about the show. It was connected to a legacy far older, and far wiser than my juvenile self: Jesus was pulling the strings like a loving master of puppets, and where that would lead was beyond my wildest dreams.

After that first show I prayed and pondered over where we should have a debut performance for a more general audience.

I realized the best place to perform this was where I worked—in the anarchist theater. I knew that before we offered to perform for someone else's community in Brazil that we should first test it in our own country, so we would understand the implications of publicly performing a show so overtly about God.

The theater hosted a monthly variety show called The Romp, where anyone was invited to perform music, spoken word, pagan rituals, and whatever else they wanted to do. I called the owner of the theater and asked her if I could perform my show about Jesus. She expressed intrigue and replied, "Yes of course, we love controversy."

I hoped my show would have equal opportunity and be treated no differently than the others. All good intellectual art is about some kind of statement and everyone is an evangelist for something the moment they open their mouth and speak what they believe. So why should mine be received any differently, especially in a theater that preached so much tolerance?

The night before the performance, I rode my bike unaccompanied to the theater and anointed it with bike grease and prayed over it. I wasn't too familiar with how anointing stuff worked, I just wanted to claim that ground for Jesus and I didn't have any holy olive oil. There was also a prayer chain going through the night in anticipation of the show.

The following day felt ominous and uncertain, as if sitting on the brink of a huge storm, just waiting for night to fall and for our time to come. My performing troupe of two and a few friends met to pray and then together we rode our bikes down to the West Bank of Minneapolis.

As we approached the venue, it appeared to be emptying. I felt a heavy attack come over my spirit that was saying, "What if this is for only a couple of people?" In reality, the people departing were just being dismissed from a rehearsal. To regain my composure we went across the street to pray again, and when we returned the theater was packed!

We would be the seventh out of nine acts and right before us was a ceremonial skit making a mockery of God and Christianity. I had seen these types of pagan performances before, and even though their message was alarmingly blasphemous, I was intensely and emotionally moved, but I wasn't offended, repulsed, scared, or upset. All I could feel was how much God loved these very people—no matter what terrible insults they hurled at Him or those who believed in Him. It felt like a perfect set up for what was about to happen.

As we waited on deck I recollected that people had their suspicions about our show. Just a few acts earlier I talked outside with one eager theatregoer, and he asked me if I was doing a puppet show with Bible verses in it. He said he had been warned about coming, but that he would take his chances. I chuckled and told him that I hoped it worked out for him.

We assembled our mini-theater in a dressing room, and as soon as it was our turn we carried it to the main stage like a coffin being brought to its grave. The theater organ music was going and then our show began. It wasn't more than a minute before the mockery and beer cans began to come flying from people in the audience. "F*** God...F*** Christianity...boring... Who wants to hear about Jesus anyway?"—were some of the insults we received. But through all of that, and the challenge of untangling puppet strings with trembling hands, I could hear some people telling others to show some respect and be quiet.

Nearing the end of the show the banter let up and I had a sense of relief over the safety of my heirloom marionettes. The show concluded and the mini-theater lights faded. Some people applauded, others booed. I had rehearsed some closing remarks for after the show and was determined to share them unless we were pulled off stage. I stood up and began to explain what the show was about. I told the audience that, "I realize many of you didn't like it, but I wanted to show you because we are taking it to Brazil and—" Then all of a sudden, the most outspoken person against us came forward to challenge me. He began to verbally attack us and not allow me to talk. Other people began to join in and a total uproar started. Then he hollered, "Who gave you permission to bring this here?" An owner of the venue stood up and said, "Actually I invited them to be here, so if you have any problems you can take them up with me." Another person stood up and said, "I think the show f****** rocked!" and that person led an applause.

I really wanted to talk about grace and how valuable every person is to God, but when the first shouting match ended a second uproar began, and another owner of the venue stepped forward to calm everyone down. My final words ended up being, "If you have questions about the show, this probably isn't the best place to discuss them. I'll be outside if you want to talk."

The theater owners escorted us off stage to the dressing room. We immediately began to disassemble the stage and chatted with the venue workers. We were concerned that they might be upset so we worked quickly to pack up in order to avoid more confrontations. To our surprise, people from the audience were filing into the backstage to thank us and congratulate us on our show and courage! They had heard my heart when I shared why I would do this, and what I believed about Jesus. There were two more acts to follow and we went outside to wait for the end of the show.

When the final Romp performance wrapped up, people gathered outside and person after person approached us with questions. They were fully open to hear me out and congratulated me on a good performance and poise in how I handled the situation considering what I was representing. I was able to share Jesus in a new way with people one-on-one.

Another notable occurrence from that night included a comment made by the closing band. Just before their first song, the lead singer said, "We don't care what people say, that puppet show f****** rocked!" Some people came over to me just to give me a hug. Later the members of the first act came over to me and said they would like to talk with me sometime about the meaning of the show. One of the guys that had escorted me off stage exclaimed, "That just made theater history!" To his knowledge this was the most controversial performance ever, which was quite a feat considering the theater thrived on controversy. He said, "Next time I'll invite you to perform again and let me know if I can help you put on another Christian puppet show."

The crowd began to disperse and it was really late into the night, but the guy who had been so angry with us was still hanging around. I knew him from working at the Seward Café together, and I had noticed several people talking to him on my behalf. I thought I should go over to him and see if I can talk it out. It didn't work.

The walls to his heart were too hard to climb over. The Holy Spirit was there and on my tongue that night, but when it came to him, it felt as if I would have to take this beating and accept defeat for the kingdom. I left on terrible terms with him and he told me that he would do whatever he could to forbid the show from happening ever again. He said he wished he had never met me. I tried to show him love in return for his anger, but he would not have it. I finally left and went home because it didn't feel safe anymore.

We had prayed that the night would send a shudder through the punk scene, and it absolutely did. People were asking, "Why was this show so controversial in a place that is normally so tolerant to everything?" "The show could have been about any other subject matter, and people wouldn't have cared, but what was it about Jesus that made people so upset?" We prayed that God would move, and He did. The show opened people's eyes to their own hate and their own lack of tolerance—which doesn't compare to God's version of tolerance when it comes to all of us; a message that urges us to "love our enemies and pray for those who hurt us."

For several years, I continued to work at that theater and attend their shows regularly. A few attendees of my show grew a fondness for my work, while others hated me. It felt strange to walk around my home city and have people talk about me behind my back. My life was never the same because wherever I went, people knew what I represented and either mocked or respected me for it. I could not remain anonymous. People would walk up to me and ask, "Are you going to ever do another Christian puppet show?" I would reply by honestly stating, "Maybe,"–and then one day, I did.

I brought a handful of friends to do a shadow theater show based on a classic children's book from 1964, Shel Silverstein's beloved story, *The Giving Tree*.

We arrived at the venue and were told beforehand that we would be the second performing act. My hopes were overall high as I deduced most of the audience would still be sober so early in the set, but the tradeoff would probably be a smaller audience. I requested a later timeslot and the venue offered us the middle slot. This would provide us with peak attendance and an audience that was not too intoxicated. We would go on right after the Psychic Sluts.

As the night progressed it was interesting to talk with people who had seen my previous puppet show. They suspiciously inquired, "What are you doing *this* time?" I just smiled and told them, "*The Giving Tree.*"

Finally it was our turn, so we pulled the shadow stage up front while it dismantled itself. My friends quickly tried to duct tape it together. Our nerves were shaky so I began to play the accordion quietly to soothe the crowd and buy us some extra time. As we continued to fix our stage we could tell the crowd was growing impatient. Some began to yell out "I hate puppets!" so I stood near them and began to nonchalantly joke with them as I tried to keep the peace. I felt like David with his harp, trying desperately to soothe King Saul from his torment— only this time the harp was an accordion and I was desperately attempting to placate 200 anxious anarchists!

Finally the stage was reassembled and the Master of

Ceremonies was ready to introduce us. "A parable of sorts," he proclaimed, and he hyped up the crowd, suggesting to them: "take yourself back to a time when you once laid in bed as your grandmother read a story." I thought, "This is perfect, a great delivery." The crowd cheered, and we began. The performance began with the hum of my accordion and the sound of this lone instrument was almost drowned out by the clapping and stomping of the audience as they began to enthusiastically join with the music. "This is great," I thought, "but how long can it last?"

Much of the audience was familiar with the story from *The Giving Tree*; they had read it as children, loved it, and probably accepted the common interpretation that the tree was Mother Earth. Throughout the story, a tree lovingly gives itself to the boy's irrational and selfish demands, but in reality "Mother Earth" does not freely give. There is always a compromise when resources are taken from the earth. The concept of the earth being the ultimate giver never sat well with me because above it is a loving Creator who created the tree.

I reimagined the story as *The Giving Tree & Taking Boy* and in my performance the tree had characteristics of a loving father and a voice representative of Jesus. I was convinced that the crowd would become enraged when the tree began to talk, but they didn't. In fact, their reaction was quite the opposite. They began to have empathy for the tree, and yell at the boy for being so selfish. I couldn't believe it! They were cheering for Jesus, and booing down the boy who was a representation of humanity.

We continued with the show and at the end we received a huge applause. The response was in extreme contrast to our prior show. Following this performance it felt as if I had received a red carpet rolled out in adoration. As we all stood to take a bow, I waited for the Master of Ceremonies to come out and introduce the next act, but he didn't. He waited. It was as if he knew I wanted space to preach and he was giving me time to do it.

The crowd grew silent when they saw that I wanted to say something and I faced my window of opportunity. There I was. I had the attention and admiration of the same crowd that had booed me off stage last time. I wanted to take that opportunity to offer a short explanation on the story as it related to Jesus, but as I stepped up, my rehearsed message was gone. I drew a total blank. There were only a couple of words that came to my mind and they were so simple. But I offered them up anyway. "Just like the boy in the story, you are not a problem." Some people yelled, "What? Say it again! We didn't hear you." I tried to say something else more related to the cross like I had rehearsed before the performance, but I could only repeat myself. "We're not a problem!" I yelled.

There was a brief silence, then the whole crowd cheered repeating back, "Yeah, we're not a problem!" That was the end of it. We told the audience that we loved them and took another bow. Then we pulled our props off stage and waited around to talk to people afterwards.

I felt relieved but also deflated. I wondered why I had not remembered what I had prepared to say. I had wanted to combat the lies that they had been told all their lives from their parents and society, concerning Mother Earth, and let them know that they are not a problem, so much that God would give His life for our debt, even though we didn't deserve it! But the words didn't come. Did I not pray hard enough? I had a perfect window, and all I said was, "We're not a problem." What stopped me?

Then I stopped and realized how selfish I was being. God could have given me different words if He wanted to. He used a donkey to speak on his behalf to Balaam in the book of Numbers. He must have known what He was doing in my case as well. I didn't see the whole picture, and the rest of the night proved that very point, as it was full of incredible conversations about the tree, and what I really wanted to say, only on an individual basis.

To unwind, and only for a moment, I left to get coffee at

a nearby cafe, and was shocked to return to see The Romp performers with bloody lips and an environment of panic and confusion. Backstage I learned that The Romp was in chaos. "We've lost the attention of the crowd," someone told me. Half the audience was outside talking, and the remaining half was intoxicated and decided to turn on the performers. All the actors were scared to return to the stage, and as they nursed their wounds they struggled to understand why beer cans had been thrown at them. I asked about what had happened, and someone replied, "After your show, the audience changed. Something was unleashed." It was requested that I help calm the crowd down with some music (since it was suggested the incident was the fault of my show). I declined at first, but they persisted and I reluctantly complied and played a waltz on the piano for a couple people who would dance. That helped appease the crowd enough so that the actors could safely perform their last act—a five-minute movie skit based on *The Wizard of Oz*.

Even in hindsight I don't entirely understand what happened that night. I do know the venue housed a serious spiritual presence about it, and with the first show we sent a shudder through the scene. But this time? Only God knows what really happened and what kind of impact our show had in the spiritual realms that gripped that place. One thing that did strike me was this: these people aren't numbers, they are relationships—and God loves these people way more than I could ever imagine.

A few days later, I was approached by someone who had been in the audience for the show and she wanted to talk. She said a friend of hers was wondering what I meant when I said, "We're not a problem." I explained my meaning and after I talked to her for a while, I asked if she had been in the audience for my first show a year prior. She shared that she was there, remembered the message of the show, and admitted she had even thrown a beer can at us that night. "What a miracle!" I thought. Over the past year, with all the shows, all the romps, and all the drinking to haze her memory, this girl remembered the message and was still contemplating what it meant for her.

This underground scene of punks, anarchists, hippies, and outliers of society will always have a special place in my heart. For this reason I continue to send my shows where groups like these gather. In 2008, I sent my heirloom marionettes to the Rainbow Gathering in a national forest to preach the gospel to a bunch of hippies. I have lead and mentored multiple walking installations at the May Day Parade in Minneapolis that is put on by the *Heart of the Beast Theater* to celebrate the coming of spring and other pagan rituals. This parade attracts the attention of over 40,000 people every year. We performed at the Full Moon Puppet Show, which was a punk rock puppet cabaret, where we saw people open to hearing the message of Jesus; people I would have never expected expressed interest and had soft hearts and open ears to hear. We also did a show at the Hard Times Café, various cabarets, and multiple times at an art crawl called Art-A-Whirl. During the 2020 Coronavirus quarantine, God led us into an encampment for people experiencing homelessness in our neighborhood park where we partnered with the leadership, started a bible study, did a couple of performances, helped a family find permanent housing, and others find a relationship with Jesus –even while theaters were all closed.

If I can escape being blacklisted, and keep people intrigued by the art of this forbidden puppet show, then I will. Jesus loves the people of this city so much. They are worth killing my artistic career for. My goal is not to cause a riot, contrary to some speculation–but to show them how much the Creator cares about them again and again and again and again and again, no matter the cost to my reputation. I am an indigenous messenger of Jesus Christ to the city of Minneapolis for as long as I am allowed to be.

INTO A BROTHEL

TOLD BY PHILIP SHOREY

———————— ◆ ————————

(2005)

SOON AFTER THE first public show at *The Bedlam*, I traveled to Brazil with members of the Scally-Waggin Circus. I was attending the Institute of Production and Recording in Minneapolis to follow my dream to one day become a film composer, and it was spring break.

The trunk had survived its maiden voyage overseas; however, the flight 10 days later back to United States became a challenging adventure. Apparently my marionette theater was one component shy of a bomb, and the newly formed TSA didn't know what to do about it.

Upon arriving in Sao Paulo, Brazil I was picked up from the airport with my Suitcase Sideshow. I was given a little time to eat and get some cash from an ATM, but only moments later, I set off with a group of Christian women on their routine walk through the city. Our plan was to pray, as they often did and let the Spirit guide our paths.

Along our walk we encountered a transvestite prostitute who was in desperate need of help. We were told that there had been a fight with their pimp, and that the whole apartment was a mess; due to the language barrier, I didn't comprehend the extent of the situation.

When we walked into the apartment, on my left were bunk beds full of ill-stricken transvestites sleeping naked and directly before me was a bloodstained tile wall. The person that had led us here was in a desperate situation; begging for our help to clean up the blood from the walls and floor, because the pimp might return soon and they didn't want his rage to be reignited by this mess that would trigger his memory of the fight.

With haste, and no protective equipment, we got on our hands and knees and began thoroughly scrubbing the walls and floors with water and a mop. We cleaned it the best we could with their supplies. Then, as we were cleaning, we learned it was the transvestite's birthday. This was cause to celebrate, regardless of the situation we found ourselves in, so one of the church ladies went out and bought a cake, and we all sang happy birthday after the horrific cleaning job was over.

I was in shock. Only a few hours prior I had traveled from the United States, I was jet lagged, and it was my first time in Brazil. Now, there I was, cleaning blood off the walls of an apartment that belonged to a group of prostituted transvestites and then throwing a party. Then it hit me. This is what Jesus did. Without any latex gloves to protect Him from human sin, corruption, and dirt, God came to us and served humbly, even unto death on the cross. He forfeited His own safety and wellbeing, and calls us to do the same.

My adventures in Brazil continued to be wild and unexpected. Like my grandparents, who travelled throughout Canada and the US, and my parents, who travelled to remote villages in Alaska, I was determined to get the show and its message as far and wide as possible. We performed for some kids sniffing glue on the streets of Sao Paulo, and we performed at makeshift venues including churches, an orphanage, the Rock Galleria, a slum named "Little Crocodile," a birthday party, and someone's house. Every show presented a unique move of God and made an impression on me, but the time that was the most memorable was certainly the shows in the 234 Brothel in the city of Sao Paulo.

The night before the brothel shows I had a long conversation with my leaders and expressed that I was fearful. I had never gone into a prostitution house and my ideas of one had all been fabricated from scenes in Hollywood movies. I imagined the pimps to be tall skinny dudes with guns that prohibited visitors that were not there to buy sex. We were going to be visiting for quite a different reason.

The group that headed to the brothel the following afternoon included three of us to perform the puppet show, a female translator, and another woman who had a friendship with some of the pimps. These two women were part of a local church that visited this particular brothel on a regular basis to foster community with prostitutes and their pimps. These faithful and fearless women were working tirelessly to help free the captives from this lifestyle and now we were all hoping the puppet show would present their constant and loving message in a fresh way.

As I left my fellow Scallywags to walk inside, I was overcome by grief because it might have been the last time I would see the outside world, or my friends again—but then I felt a warm peace fill my spirit. I was actually following Jesus into the brothel. I wondered, "Will this be the end or could we lead a mass exodus if we come out alive?"

We walked into the entry-level floor to ask the first pimp for permission to perform the show. The brothel was located in an apartment building and every floor was run by a different female pimp who my translator referred to as cheas. What the chea said was law. We weren't sure if we would perform the show once, repeatedly, or not at all. It completely depended on what the cheas allowed, and this was unexpected for me because my impression of how a prostitution house might be run did not include little old ladies as the pimps. For some reason it made the whole situation to me even more heartbreaking. Here were women selling other women into sexual slavery, and to them, it was just a way to make a living.

My translator explained the show to the first chea and she agreed to let us perform. Then we began to set it up. Some of the ladies stood near us, but others continued to work and were not permitted to attend. The prostitutes were assigned to their respective floors and wings. They did not have permission to wander about the apartment complex. If they were going to see the show we would have to go to them.

Each floor and wing were in competition with the others as men entered the building and walked up the stairwell looking at the "merchandise" to be purchased off a sad sort of display. The working ladies stood, mostly naked, throughout the stairwell, and half-heartedly pulling on our clothes until they realized we weren't there to do business. It was an utterly dark and depressing place.

As we were performing the first show, the room began to fill. There were five people in our audience and after the show I shared a few words about how much value they had to God. The women seemed receptive and open, but it didn't seem to sink in. I thought to myself, "Well, the show does speak for itself, and the impact of foreign men presenting a show in Jesus' name, without asking for anything in return, might speak louder than anything I could ever say."

As I turned around, my translator approached me with news. "A pimp upstairs wants you to do the show for her ladies right away." We obediently gathered our stage and props and went to the next floor of the brothel.

Upstairs I was able to meet the second chea. I felt the Holy Spirit come over me strongly as I began setting up the stage. I was fighting off tears. There were nearly twenty women who were present to watch the show.

As we performed the show, sweat was dripping from my forehead to the floor of the stage. When the show ended, I came out from behind the stage and spoke of how big God is and that nothing is too difficult for Him. I spoke of how much grace He has for us; He even extended grace to a murderer who once hunted down Christians. Then I asked if anyone wanted prayer. The chea came forward and declared, "I would like you to pray for all my women, that they would find a way out of this place." So they all came forward and gathered in a circle. As I prayed for them in English, others translated my prayers into Portuguese, and then more prayers were offered up and these too were translated.

After that show we were able to talk with the women and learn their names and even offer information for future support. Then we were told that the chea in the adjacent wing wanted us to do the show for her ladies too! We picked up the stage and props and dragged them across the hall and set it up for the next group. This third chea told the ladies that she wanted all of them to stop whatever they were doing, and if they were with any men as customers for business they would have to wait and watch the puppet show with them first.

Can you imagine that?! Walking into a brothel and expecting to meet a prostitute, but finding yourself required to see a puppet show about Jesus? I even witnessed this happen as a male customer and his selected prostitute were stopped from going into the back room and instead directed to sit down and watch our performance first.

We finished setting up for show number three. The stage was starting to break apart by now. We had some technical issues, during the performance but we made it through, and at the end of the show I spoke again of who God is and that He created all of us with a purpose to glorify Him. I said we would love to pray with anyone who would like to know Him. All the ladies and the chea wanted prayer so we stood up and prayed together.

One of my fellow puppeteers talked and prayed with one of the ladies. As they stood together and prayed, they both began to sob. I even started to cry because I could feel the healing power that was beginning to happen in her heart. I will never forget what I saw in that moment. It was like a glimpse of God's broken heart was being fastened onto my heart and it was changing who I was forever. I was able to see a glimpse of God's brokenhearted love for these women that transcended what the world sought to destroy and what they looked like on the outside. I just couldn't believe all that was happening. We said our goodbyes to the women on that floor and then I was told that we had received a green light to perform the show on another floor.

Once again we packed the stage and this time we put it in the elevator. This floor seemed a lot more crowded with people than the others. There were men and women everywhere leaning against the walls, sitting on benches and standing wherever there was room. We were directed to set up in a small corner of the room. There was a spiritual darkness on this floor, which was run by a chea who was a witch doctor and practiced Macumba, a form of African witchcraft.

Little gift offerings to "dark spirits" were hanging on the walls all above us, and our Christian guides had struggled in the past to build a relationships here because of the spiritual conflict they had with the witch doctor. The witch doctor was vocal about her distain for Christians—but she was apparently okay with a puppet show and didn't want her workers to miss out on the entertainment the others had received. This opportunity to perform the show was a miracle.

After this fourth performance, I offered the same message that God had placed on my heart. I shared that if anyone wanted prayer, that we would love to pray with them. Everybody wanted prayer. The women from the adjacent wing were straining to watch the show from down the hall, and they yelled that they wanted to pray as well. I asked everyone who wanted to pray to stand up with me and as I prayed my translator prayed in Portuguese, and others repeated it down the hall so all the women would be able to hear.

After we concluded that fourth show, we were told it was time to leave. We had been there for several hours and the ride for the puppet stage was waiting. We broke the stage down a final time and collected more names and information of the women who wanted follow-up care. The women expressed gratitude for our visit and even the men were thanking us as we departed. A woman seemed to be only half joking when she said, "I'll fit in the suitcase, just get me out of here." I felt like crying. It was actually really hard to leave because I wanted so desperately to take them *all* with me. Maybe it could have happened. I don't know. I did what I set out to do in the brothel, but in hindsight my faith still wasn't where I wish it could have been.

That evening we walked out of the 234 Brothel after praying with over forty prostitutes as a result of a puppet show presenting a Bible story. This encouraged the local church and enhanced their relationships with the people in the brothel. It was at that moment that I heard God speak to me and say, "This little traveling marionette theater has a place on the global missions stage." It wasn't an audible voice, but a strong sense I felt in my inner-core. It became evident that God could get the glory through this simple production.

That spring break trip in 2005 wrecked me for an ordinary life, and I realized I wasn't studying to become a film composer anymore. I knew that if a career in music wasn't God's plan for my life, I didn't want anything to do with it. I still felt called to finish school, but somehow I wanted to use art to change the world, not just climb a Hollywood career ladder. The world didn't need another celebrity or blockbuster film to allow moviegoers to avoid reality for a few hours. What the world needed was Jesus! Playing the Hollywood rat-race couldn't compare to what God could do with my little loaves and fishes (in the form of marionettes) if I were to completely surrender my plans to Him, *kill my art*, and learn to collaborate with the Creator of the universe.

I graduated from IPR in the spring of 2006, and was given two life-changing opportunities. I could either work on a big budget documentary film with a Hollywood film composer, or tour Europe with No Longer Music and be discipled by

David Pierce. For me it was a no-brainer. I chose to forgo my Hollywood dream and instead toured Europe to grow in my calling as an evangelistic artist. I never looked back. It's been the ride of a lifetime.

CURB SIDE JESUS PROJECT

TOLD BY PHILIP SHOREY

————————◆————————

(2005 - 2007)

AFTER MY SHORT trip to Brazil, I felt inspired by the work that was being done there with the marginalized. I was unwilling to settle back into a normal life. Then one day, I was riding my bicycle and noticed a group of Native Americans flying a sign by a highway off-ramp. The image of wandering Sao Paulo, Brazil, while being available for any opportunity to love others flashed back to me. I recalled how God used the ministry of the local church-women to unite us with a transvestite prostitute who they could serve.

Several people from my local church, *The Salvage Yard*, were also involved in a mobile serving ministry called *The Jesus Kitchen*. Volunteers for *The Jesus Kitchen* would set up across the street from The Hard Times Café and at national Rainbow Gatherings. There they would serve food and have meaningful conversations with the people they encountered. The idea came to me to start a similar ministry and I called it the *Curb Side Jesus Project*.

Participation in the *Curb Side Jesus Project* simply involved being available and open to serve whomever God would choose to show us while taking a consistent route on a bike ride every week. A group of two or three would ride together and visit the people standing on the highway exit ramps of Minneapolis. In the winter, we offered hearty hot soup and in the summer we had ice water on hand. I didn't want to take the easy route and serve junk food, because Jesus doesn't serve us junk, so on one special occasion I brought a camp stove and cooked steak beside the exit ramp. I offered Bibles and local resource books for people experiencing homelessness. Of course, while my intention was to present the Gospel to those in the street much like my great-grandfather had done in Canada with The Salvation Army, God's intention was also to build my understanding of poverty and inspire me through these experiences to write a new story that would travel with The Suitcase Sideshow.

Through the Scallywag's Bike Club, I had become heavily involved with the traveling and self-proclaimed American Gypsy* culture[25], crusty punks, and travelling kids who hopped trains. It was a deep counter-culture, full of pride, but very cool and glamorous to those lured by its promise of freedom. Some of the travelers came from terrible circumstances, but many were just looking for an adventure and an escape from their parents in suburban life. Their glory and pride was in their shame and scars, but when I began seeking out people who were really desperate for help, and who didn't want to live on the street, my heart began to break in new ways. They were truly seeking a hand up, away from their horrific situations, rather than a hand out to sustain their life-style.

I asked God to give me fresh eyes to see people who were truly looking for change and he did—I met a woman who had been a nurse. She got drunk one night, and went into work the next day with a hangover. She made one bad decision, which led to her losing her job and her nursing license. Within the week, she lost her career, experienced homelessness, and started to accumulate debt. She was so angry. After learning her story, I prayed for her like my life depended on it. She told me, "You better pray for me or I might do something else I will regret."

---

25 Roma is the ethnic name for a group of people who are derogatively referred to as Gypsy. Although the word and concept of being a Gypsy is widespread, it was errantly cultivated by people who thought that the Roma came from Egypt. It is more likely that they were a royal entertaining cast that was banished from India around 600AD. They fled through the Middle East, experienced generations of being nomadic, and were highly persecuted. Many of them settled when they arrived in Eastern Europe.[1]

I met one young man who had just lost his mom to cancer. He didn't know his dad, and he had moved to the city to go to college but his financial aid had fallen through. He was scared. He hugged me on the side of the road and started crying like I was the only soul who cared for him in the world. I tried to reassure him saying, "Listen, God loves you. He sees your pain, and he is with you if you call out to him, but right now you need to take care of your basics. I will help you with that, and as far as the street goes, don't ever call it home. It will suck you in like an institution and you could lose your drive."

I would bring the people I met to church, if they were willing, and pray with them while they were there flying their signs. Most of the time they simply desired someone to talk to. Other times they just told me to get lost.

On one occasion, I found myself begging for money to help someone I had just met. He needed money for a bus ticket home in order to start his life over. I didn't have any money, but I could help him beg and we could cover more ground if we split up. I humbled myself for a few minutes, asking people for money to help a friend, and it broke my heart as I saw how a person begging for money feels and is treated and stereotyped by society. He did manage to get home and off the streets, but a few years later I heard the devastating news that a relapse to heroin had claimed his life.

Experiences like these added to the urgency I felt to tell more people about Christ's healing love and drove me to create a third show. This new performance would need to touch on the human issues of brokenness, healing, and celebration while portraying Jesus as the hero. The show developed into three acts that included a scene for a man experiencing homelessness, a prostitute, and a corporate CEO or politician. There was also a creepy religious opening to introduce the villain. These stories were modern day retellings of the biblical stories, respectively, of the leper (Matthew 8:1-4), Mary Magdalene (John 8:1-8), and the tax collector (Matthew 9:9-13). I named the finished production *Blessed are the Poor.*

This new show was very intense and I quickly learned that it always worked better if there was a trust established through a relationship. A show with this kind of substance that provokes heavy questions should be handled delicately. When I travel, I depend on the relationships from locals that I'm working with, but when I'm at home I have sometimes spent years volunteering at homeless shelters or visiting people under bridges in hopes of building that same trust for sharing my show. I have wrestled with the notion of doing good deeds with an agenda, but have come to recognize that my sincere desire is to show the greatest message of love I can possibly show them.

I also learned to be keen on finding the "Man of Peace" as mentioned by Jesus in Luke 10:6, "When you enter a new town, look for the man of peace." This is the man or woman who has influence and respect in the community. If you find favor with this person, then the Holy Spirit will lead you to other people who are under their influence. My parents and grandparents found this "Man of Peace" in the churches they would visit. I, on the other hand, had the challenge of trying to find this unique person in unusual places.

I had become friends with some Native American tribe members and one particular community that was deep in the drug scene. They were living under a bridge by the Walker Art Center. Within this community there was a man I had met who seemed different from anyone else. He seemed completely unfettered by his surroundings and living situation. Over time we became close and I learned that he had faith in Jesus. We were good for each other because he wanted his friends to come to receive Christ, but he needed accountability and encouragement to kick the addictive sins in his life that had led him to experience homelessness.

Sometimes I wondered if he was voluntarily sabotaging his sobriety so that he would have to remain among the people that he loved—but other times I knew he was truly struggling with the sin that kept him there. Jesus had shown me that he was the "Man of Peace" regardless of his own personal battle with sin, and I knew God still desired to work through him. Eventually I gained enough courage to ask the community if I could perform my new show for them in their camp.

The night before the scheduled performance, I went down to the bridge to pray and make sure everything was set. Being at a camp for those experiencing homelessness—it's completely unstable and typical for the unexpected to happen all the time, but it seemed like we would be able to pull this off. People were excited about the show and my friend, the "Man of Peace," told me that I needed to do an altar call after the show. I shook with joy when he said that because I wanted to, but wasn't sure how, or what that would look like under a bridge. He said he felt certain someone would give their life to Jesus that night, and I took that word as the confirmation I needed. My faith for God to move powerfully is always bolstered by the faith of men and women who are part of the community receiving the show. I imagine it was the same for my parents and grandparents.

The next afternoon myself and a few friends arrived at the location, under the bridge, and the whole camp was in chaos. There had recently been a fight and the Minneapolis Police Department was attempting to remove people from under the bridge. People were on high alert and running around. I tried finding the "Man of Peace," but he was nowhere to be found. There was so much going on, it was hard to get a full story, but we set up the stage and started serving soup and giving out warm clothes anyway. For some reason The Suitcase Sideshow seems to thrive in chaos.

A few people stayed and gathered around after they ate, but not the whole camp like we were hoping. Finally it was time to make a decision. Will we do the show or not? We prayed about it, and then decided that the show must go on, even if it is just for a small audience. We made the final announcement that the show would be starting in 10 minutes. A large intoxicated man joined the audience and halfway through the show his friend with red hair and a flannel shirt also sat down to watch. The intoxicated man was quite rowdy, but the man with the flannel shirt, who had also eaten and hung out with us that afternoon, seemed really into the show.

The performance went pretty smooth, but I kept a keen eye over the curtain to watch for the unexpected. Afterwards I came out to explain a few things and invited people to ask Jesus into their lives. The man in flannel stood up right away, but his intoxicated friend tried pulling him back down. As he shook his friend off he said to me, "It's not his time yet. It's my time." So we stood together and talked and then prayed while he received Christ.

Afterwards some more of the camp residents came down and we chatted. They apologized that they missed the show and then started to really open up to us about their lives. We got a chance to pray for one of the women and share more food. The "Man of Peace" did not show up, but I later learned his brother was there watching the show and he told me more about their situation.

For a while, we regularly continued to visit the community under the bridge and offer resources and share the message of God's love and a hope for a new life. I did this until I had an opportunity to go on a European tour with The Suitcase Sideshow. Upon my return to Minneapolis, I went to pay a visit but the people I had known from before had been forced to move on. The city fenced up the former site of the camp to prevent anyone from living under that bridge, and it is still fenced up to this present day.

As I inquired around town about the whereabouts of my friends the response from others in the homeless community were, "They left." "They got off the street." "They went home to get a job and see their family," and, "They moved south." Thus was the unexpected ending of that chapter. I had planted a seed and had to trust that God would see it through to fruition. It was someone else's turn to be Jesus to them.

To this day, I still have the itch to do this kind of God-directed city-exploration like I experienced in Brazil. I try to be open to make space in my day-to-day life for God to prompt and direct me. But how cool would it be, to do this again, and with others? What if more of the church went on bicycle rides, not just to see cool things, get exercise, or hang out by a fire on the Mississippi River; but to deliver food, prayer, water, aid, and hope to those who need it and are living on the streets? What if we dedicated one day a month or week to bike around the city, get some exercise, have some fun, and bless some really hungry people in Jesus' name? What do you think would happen to the community of those experiencing homelessness? What do you think would happen to the local church?

TRIALS OF TRANSYLVANIA

TOLD BY PHILIP SHOREY

———————◆———————

(2006 - 2010)

IN THE LATE summer of 2006, I flew from Istanbul, Turkey to Bucharest, Romania. I had spent the first part of the summer touring with the evangelistic rock opera No Longer Music as an actor and video DJ. The tour started in Poland performing in squats and being threatened by skinheads, and the last leg of the tour was in the Middle East where the secret police were constantly on our tails. The journey was exhausting, but thrilling. I had learned much and had seen God move powerfully across cultures. It had reopened my eyes to the radical life of living by faith and using art to present the Gospel in revolutionary ways, but now after the final show and heartfelt goodbyes, it was time to set out on my own and put what I had learned to the test. Although the mentoring I had just been given was imperative, nothing would compare and test me more than going through the trials of Transylvania.

While mid-flight to Romania, I met a man on the airplane who was a Turkish Muslim. He was very impressed with my devotion to God. He told me that he wished every Muslim loved God as much as I did. When we landed, he assisted me by calling a taxi to help me get to the train station. My intended itinerary was to get on a train headed for Debrecen, Hungary, where I had hopeful leads for getting my show *The Story of Saul's Conversion* translated and recorded into Hungarian and Romanian.

When I arrived at the train station, I was robbed by the taxi driver and forced to give him all my money. I was now penniless and all I had was a credit card that I wasn't sure would work. At that point a man offered to help me find the right counter to buy my ticket. I trailed him to the proper window, not because of his leading, but because that was where the signs pointed. As I waited in the ticket queue, he stayed beside me and began crying and begging for money. I was so confused. He continued wailing but when I insisted that I had nothing to help him with, he abruptly stopped crying and walked away like nothing had happened. This was my first encounter with manipulative begging which is a stereotype of the Roma people.

I was able to purchase my ticket with my credit card, and it felt like a miracle. Then I made a phone call to my contact in Hungary. During this conversation I learned that due to a festival in the city there was no room to rent in Debrecen, and that everyone my contacts knew were too busy with a Good Sports soccer camp to record my show into Hungarian. Hearing this after being robbed by a taxi driver and my encounter with a dramatic beggar left me feeling defeated. I walked warily onto the platform towards my train and then paused to sigh. As I paused, I saw to my left across a few platforms, a weathered orthodox man sitting on a bench and wearing a worn suit and sagging fedora. He was waiting for a train and was hunched over while clutching onto a large golden cross. It seemed as if he held on to the cross like it was his last hope. I saw reflected in him the desperation for God that I needed to be reminded of at that very moment. If I was going to see God move in Transylvania, Jesus was my only hope.

I boarded my train and headed for Debrecen, Hungary. After settling into my seat I recollected the shows that I had just done with No Longer Music and all the obstacles we had faced—which had included being threatened by the secret police in Istanbul and skin-heads in Poland—yet, God always provided for us and paved the way for hundreds of people to hear the Gospel and receive Jesus into their lives. I could have easily become disheartened when the trials came, but I took these obstacles as encouragement, knowing that there were going to be spiritual armies against me hoping to stop the message from getting through. But God was with me and He would somehow make a way through a miracle.

During the night, my train passed through several small mountain villages. I made failed attempts to blend in and became quite curious about this impoverished country full of legends and folklore. Some local students spoke with me in their broken English and I learned from them that most people here felt trapped by a hopeless economic situation. I wanted to help them find peace, and bring an answer for their poverty, but all I could do was listen, learn, and try to believe God was bigger than the adversity and hardships experienced as a result of Romanian political corruption.

Early the next day I reached the stop for my destination of Debrecen, Hungary. The morning air was chilly, but waiting for me at the station was a missionary from Texas named Russell Chun who was, at first glance, not very impressed with me. He graciously found me a place to stay where I discovered authentic Hungarian hospitality at its finest—pig fat (szalonna), onions, and bread around a campfire. Then he proceeded to call our mutual friends in the USA to reconfirm that I was legitimate and trustworthy. While helping me plan this part of my trip these friends had spoken very highly of me, but I had shown up quite smelly, with long shaggy hair, holes in my clothes, and worst of all, in dirty unkempt military combat boots. As Russell (a military veteran) expressed his uncertainties, they upheld their recommendation and said, "Yes, he's the real deal. Give him a chance."

It started with this encounter, and continued through other similar experiences in Transylvania, where I learned that I didn't want to be an evangelist for crusty punk style or post-modern culture. If fashion was going to be the overwhelming focal point in how people perceived me, I needed to work on being less true to my image and more true to Jesus so that when I left, they remembered more about Jesus, and less about how I looked or smelled.

Thankfully, and despite my road weary appearance, the local church (including Russell) was incredibly supportive. They set aside time during the soccer camp so we were able to translate and record the show into both Hungarian and Romanian. I told them that someday I would return. I don't know if they actually believed me, but having to turn down other touring opportunities to keep my word, I returned the following year in 2007 with two dear friends (Andrew and Katie Dirks), a marionette theater, and a word of caution that the Dirks might need to cover up their tattoos.

The first place we performed was in a town called Miskolc. Russell and his family had a compassionate and long-term commitment to an orphanage in this town and had even adopted a little girl from there. They loved those kids and visited them regularly to play baseball and talk to them about God's love.

We set up our show on the grass in the shaded courtyard of the orphanage and I knew God wanted to do something big, but I also knew that I was in way over my head in a culture I did not understand. I felt like Aragorn who was destined to be king in *The Lord of the Rings*, but overcome by the fear of failing in a major way. I was afraid of what God was leading me to do.

During the performance, most of the cool kids watched our show from the back. They were somewhat skeptical of a puppet show, but as the show progressed they warmed up to us and the Holy Spirit must have been speaking to them.

After the show I gave an offer to come up and accept Jesus but nobody moved. In faith, I asked a second time and could feel the spiritual battle and tension raging in the orphanage. The fear of peer pressure and approval hung like a thick cloud keeping everyone in their place. Finally I asked, "Who will be the leader and let go of what others think and take this radical step to know God?" One by one the older kids came up followed by the younger kids. Eventually the whole orphanage was kneeling with me in prayer and asking Jesus into their lives in the middle of the grass. Russell was in shock. He had never imagined this happening and couldn't believe a crusty punk kid with unkempt combat boots could ever be used by God in this way. He phoned his wife to tell her what had just happened, grinning ear to ear.

It was truly a testament of how the Body of Christ can embrace diversity, learn from different members and do what the other parts couldn't. Like iron sharpening iron, I saw God grow our working friendship over the years and the beauty was that as I had learned to surrender my style to Jesus. Through Russell, Good Sports has embraced those with alternative styles and sees value in how those people can appeal to youth and even seeks it out in their leaders. If my family lineage had taught me anything at that moment, it was that God loved pushing the comfort levels of the church for the sake of outsiders finding Him; Alex with magic in the 1940s, Edgar with music in the 1960s, Shawnette with ventriloquism in the 1980s, and now me with *high* fashion in the 2000s.

We remained there the rest of the day and spent the night with the kids in the orphanage, just playing with them and talking.

The following day was Sunday, so it seemed right to all go to church. We walked to a nearby church and filed into the chairs. There were so many kids that we literally packed the place out. We were hoping the local church would help us with these young believers; however, they were so surprised that it seemed they didn't really know what to do with all of these kids. I kept them on my heart and that Christmas organized people from my church to send them some gifts. When I returned in 2010, I was told that many of the kids were still following Jesus and growing in their faith.

After that first week around Debrecen, our plan was to travel with a construction crew and perform our show alongside their efforts to build housing in Roma villages. The trip was cancelled, and I was gutted because I love it when the Gospel message gets to work in partnership with such obvious humanitarian service.

Jesus met the needs of the people spiritually *and* physically.

Russell wanted our show to continue ministering in Transylvania and sought out an opportunity for us. On very short notice he connected us with an amazing organization in Marghita, Romania. The organization was called Fundatia Crestina Elim (FCE) and it was started by folks from Sweden in the 1990s as the inhumane conditions in the Romanian orphanages were revealed to the world. They all agreed that a marionette theater would be great for the Romanian orphans and Roma people that they worked with in Transylvania.

We started our 10-day tour of Romanian shows in Borumlaca. Before setting up, we visited with the villagers for a while, played the Singing Saw, and showed them the marionettes. During this time a Roma mother came up to me and spontaneously handed me her baby. I was surprised and wasn't sure what to do. "Was the baby a gift?" I wondered. It happened so fast I didn't know how to react. I didn't even remember the last time I had held a baby. "How do you hold the head? Was it this way, or that way?" As I clumsily tried to figure out how to support this tiny body, one of the FCE women came over to me and said, "Oh what a beautiful baby" and gathered him up in her arms. Well, that was a massive relief. Later, I learned they were *not* giving me the baby to have a better life in America, but had a superstition that if I touched the baby it would be blessed.

We started setting up and intended to finish our performance before sundown because Transylvanian folklore insists that everything unruly comes alive at night. This particular village even had a reputation for chasing missionaries out after dark. Before the performance we did a demonstration to show how the marionettes operate. We had learned that seeing a marionette move for the first time can mesmerize Roma children and distract them from the overall message of the story.

After the show I shared the word God had put on my heart, which was to remind them of God's love, and that they are not a problem to God. I asked if anyone wanted to pray and receive

Jesus into their lives, and many kids came over to my side to pray. Others watched with curiosity and talked with us about it afterwards. It almost felt like a repeat to the show we did in the Miskolc orphanage.

In the days to follow, we ventured into many other places that would put our faith and emotions to the test in different ways—but the biggest test and challenge happened at a government-run institution called Cadea. Cadea housed low-functioning adults who had severely suffered while they were born under the communist reign of Nicolae Ceauşescu.

Ceauşescu's government had grandiose ambitions to build a massive army and work force—so they mandated women to birth several children for the cause. Without a healthy economy to support the rapid growth in population, babies were being left in hospitals because many parents could not afford to feed their children. These children grew up as orphans or wards of the state, and Ceauşescu's government propagated that the fetus is the property of society and they could successfully raise the children institutionally.

It was during this time, while "*The Shorey Family's Lighthouse Ministry*" was traversing the United States, that the elites of Eastern Bloc Communism were rejecting what Western psychology was unearthing about human development and a child's need for physical touch from a loving caregiver. This erroneous rejection lead an understaffed institution to chain many kids to their beds, mentally disabling a large amount of this generation of Romanian children who grew up in the 1980's and were now young adults like me.

These young adults are now housed in places like Cadea, which is where we were headed for our next show. There had been a lot of chaos amongst the staff and residents of Cadea on the morning of the show, and when we arrived at the institutional housing the scene was out of control. We stepped out of the van and were instantly swarmed by a throng of people who were either buzzing with excitement or overcome by panic.

Eventually we found ourselves lead into a big room and isolated from the chaos outside. We began asking each other, "What on earth are we going to do here? How can we put on a show in this kind of environment?" We set up the stage and prayed to God for discernment and wisdom for the performance and sensitivity of this audience.

After giving word that we were ready, we braced ourselves as a massive hysteric wave flooded the room. As everyone was finding a position in a seat or somewhere on the floor, I played a solemn melody with my Singing Saw. The music began to lull the audience and I again witnessed an effect that I can only compare to the situation where an anxious King Saul became placated by the soothing notes of David's harp. As soon as everyone settled, I quickly introduced the show and we began.

We weren't sure how this audience would react. The first half of our show was boisterous and light-hearted and would usually keep a crowd's attention, but the second half was wordy and we were concerned that it might lose them. The first half did keep their attention quite readily. The audience was in an uproar over the humor, pointing and screamed out responses and enjoyed every minute of that act. When the second half began the room became hushed and all eyes were fixed on the stage. Focus and concentration were heightened while they silently cried together watching this story of love and hope. We were shocked by the silence and felt God was in this place.

After the show I apprehensively stepped out from my post behind the stage and shared that God's love is powerful, that the audience had all been created with a purpose and that they were not a mistake! I had spoken those words many times after my shows, but in that place and at that moment, I felt the same words fall heavy with more meaning than ever before. Then with great faith, I earnestly proclaimed that the Creator of the universe sees them as valuable enough to die for on the cross! Then we all prayed together and I boldly asked if anyone had any questions.

The first person to respond cried out, "This place is too evil. God can't be here." Then another guy sprang up and began to share with everyone, "What we just saw happen to Saul in the story, can happen to us too! God changed his life! We just want to thank you for coming and bringing this reminder to us. We need to pray! We want to pray for you, and thank you, and we also want to pray for the principals here, because they don't know God, and they beat us! We need to pray that they stop beating us!" As he boldly prayed, I observed the principal staff sitting in the back began to shift and squirm uncomfortably. It was like I was back at a riotous romp in Minneapolis, but this time the crowd wasn't turning on me, it was turning on the leadership.

I now had the role of audience as another resident stood up, and said, "I want to pray too! I want to also pray that the principals would stop beating us!" After that the principals silently slipped out of the room, and as they did, everyone started screaming, "They're gone, they're gone!" We were rushed by the crowd as they showed us the scars on their arms and faces from being beaten, and shared with us their sorrow. "It was him, he did it," they told us pointing fingers towards the door where the principals departed. I gazed around as person after person came up and grabbed me to pull me towards their story of grief, anger, and struggle.

One girl, named Samona, had been beaten that day for speaking out against an injustice. With dry blood still caked on her face, she grabbed me and told me never to forget her. She thanked us for coming and said that she would be praying for us, but said again and again, "Don't forget me. When are you coming back?" I stood there and embraced her, listening to her pain, trying to understand, but unable. I wanted to cry, but couldn't. I became so overwhelmed by this trauma right in front of me that my emotional response was shutting off. All I could do was listen, and hold her. I wanted to cry tears of sorrow, but they wouldn't come.

As Samona carried on I suddenly had enough. I couldn't

process her words anymore. It was too much. I interjected and said, "I'm sorry, I can't understand what you're going through here. I have never experienced something remotely close to life in this place. I am sorry, but I can tell you this: Jesus did experience this! Just like you feel about what has happened to you unjustly, the same thing happened to Jesus. He didn't do anything wrong, but they tortured and killed him. He spoke out against the evil in this world too, and He knows what you're going through. He knows the injustice that you feel. He loves you and is angry about the pain in this world." As she eagerly nodded, I continue by telling her, "God brought us here to remind you that even in such a dark place as this, Jesus can be here with you if you ask Him to be, and He will help you." She gripped my hand and used her teeth to bite a strand of bracelet off her wrist. Then she tied it around my wrist and told me "I won't ever forget you. Don't forget about me."

Our visit to Cadea ended with an attempt to lighten the atmosphere through teaching residents how to play the Singing Saw. After leaving we found a small nearby park to decompress and process our experience. We wondered how we might possibly help this devastating situation. We discussed the challenges for people like Samona, who were abandoned as infants and then abused at the hand of their caregivers.

Unfortunately, there are many places like this throughout former Eastern Bloc countries, and many times the townspeople don't even know they exist; the government tries to keep it undercover because the history is too shameful. But God sees these forgotten children. He loves them and is deeply pained by the injustice they experienced. The residents of these institutions are the ones God talks about when he speaks of the meek, the orphan, and the poor in spirit. They may be the outcasts and underprivileged of society—but they are never forgotten or forsaken by Jesus. There is always hope, even for depressing institutions.

I saw a glimpse of this hope in Romania when at one of our street shows in a neighboring town, I recognized a Cadea staff member who came forward when I asked people to make a decision in the street to follow Jesus. It was beautiful, and this is how the change can begin.

During that summer we were unwittingly involved in sewing seeds for change in another institution. We performed a show for a handful of kids in a drab juvenile jail in Poland, and a few workers gave their lives to Jesus in response. I didn't give it a second thought—and it is always a challenge to read the sincerity of such an action—but God was orchestrating something huge. Additional workers came to faith through a No Longer Music show shortly after that, and when we returned three years later by their invitation, the whole atmosphere was different. The grey concrete walls were painted bright colors. Lovely curtains were in the windows to conceal the iron bars, and printed tablecloths were laid on the tables. The residents seemed light-hearted, and I saw a priest rocking out on the guitar as a kid played drums in his jail cell. Over tea we heard stories of how God was changing this juvenile jail and restoring people's lives. I asked them what happened here to cause such a dramatic change and they shared that God used my show and NLM to give the leadership a real heart for these kids.

This is why we do this! Healing is happening! God's heart is breaking for these kids—and if we gain even an ounce of the heart of our heavenly Dad, our hearts should break as well. Pray for these people and support those who give their lives to Christ's mission in loving the poor in Jesus's name.

After our attempt to process our most challenging Romanian show at Cadea, we continued to present shows in villages throughout the Black Forest and in additional orphanages and institutions. In response to the heaviness of the situations we were facing, our spirits were becoming desensitized and our actions began feeling calculated and robotic. I was emotionally shutting down and just going through the motions of performance. I needed additional time to process, but there was none to be found. In my heart, I was done. I had nothing left to give.

In the midst of this trial we learned that the main bridge on highway 35W over the Mississippi River in Minneapolis had just collapsed on August 1ˢᵗ. We weren't sure which of our friends and family had been affected or killed by the disaster. I was scared and drained in every possible way. But there were still more shows scheduled for us and that night we would have one at a church in a village called Popesti. I was told it was an impoverished small village, and the crowd would be distinctly rowdy.[26] The reputation of the show was attracting townspeople, orphans, and Roma from all neighboring villages because similar to where my Grandpa went in the countryside towns of Canada, and my mom in the Inuit villages of Alaska, entertainment was scarce in these remote parts of Transylvania and people craved it.

As we drove to that show, I felt a pressure in my chest and a shooting pain going down my neck. As I was achingly jostled by the bumpy roads all I could do was offer this prayer, "God, where are You!? What am I going to do tonight?"

As we pulled into the driveway of the church we were swarmed. "Nothing ever comes here," someone announced to me. This was going to be another big show and I was scared. I didn't even want to do the show, so as the others set up the stage

---

26 There is an inaccurate stereotype which promotes the idea that if a place is poor, it will also be rowdy, dangerous, and full of crime. Although edgy places usually make better stories and get in all the books, it should be brought to the attention of the reader that not every impoverished environment we have performed in has been dangerous. One time we performed on the outskirts of Constanta, Romania, in a small village near the Black Sea. The family that invited us into their neighborhood had built their home from mud bricks, using the very mud that the home sat upon. We had rarely witnessed poverty to this degree; however, the kids were incredibly well behaved, the hospitality was impeccable, the love in the home was precious, and the father had a deep sense of pride in what he was doing. This was a family of new believers who had just started attending the local church. The mission we were partnering with felt our show would be an excellent way to disciple and encourage them. This observation revealed to me the very important truth that poverty does not always equal crime and despair, rather it is more connected to the breakdown of the family which has the power to create a generational curse in any socioeconomic environment. What is the solution to reduce crime and instill morality from this observation? I would wager, through my travel experiences, that the only solution is keeping the family together and healthy, keeping a foundation of truth with Christ at the center, and giving opportunity for the next generation to succeed.

in the church, I hid in the van and unsuccessfully tried to get some rest. I watched as crowds of people began to pour into the church to see our lousy show, and I tuned into voices in my head that were repeating to me something they had been muttering for weeks: "Philip, you're going to let everybody down. Look at all these people coming to see your stupid 15-minute show. It's not even dark, so the lights won't even be seen. They probably won't even understand the story. What's the point? You can't change anything." I knew these thoughts were lies, but I was too weary to fight them off. I opened my Bible to whatever fell open like seeking a drop of water from a slow dripping water pump in the desert, because I didn't have the strength to search for something more. The pages parted and settled in Psalms. I read whatever I could, searching for life to breathe into my (what felt like) sinking spirit, but today they were just words on a page. Everything fell silent. I felt as if I was carrying the weight of the world, even though I knew that burden was not mine to hold.

In the silence, my gaze drifted to the bracelet that Samona had given me. It was like "black despair" that I might have carried to prove that I cared, but it was killing me. I slowly remove the bracelet from my wrist. It was too much for me to bear, and that was the moment I truly gave her sorrow and everything else back to Jesus for Him to handle. I acknowledged that I'm not the Messiah or any kind of hero, and I am not meant to carry that weight. Jesus already carried it on the cross along with every other pain anyone else has ever faced. I will help, but it isn't my job to save the world. I wasn't designed for that. I am just an artist and a messenger of Jesus Christ.

All too soon, my interpreter opened the door of the van and asked, "Did you get some rest? We're ready for you." I retorted, "No, of course not, but whatever. Let's do it." I pressed through the crowd in the church to get to the front of the stage. I asked the team, "What should we do first?" and they looked at me surprised because I usually have a plan. "You're asking us?" they replied. Then someone suggested, "Let's sing some worship songs." I agreed and they played a couple of songs as I accompanied with my Singing Saw. The church was packed with people and more wanted to come in, so I decided to invite everyone to come closer and even sit in the aisle. I hoped the crowd would get rowdy, because maybe it would wake me up a little and that would be helpful.

I introduced the show as I always did, but I also honestly shared that I was tired and had no energy. Throughout the show I was grabbing the wrong puppets and halfway through I thought I was going to pass out. Everything was spinning and then somehow it was over. I stepped out to wrap up the show, intended to preach, but I didn't really know what to say, so I just read something from the Bible. The passage I shared was something Paul, the main character in the show, wrote to the Church in Corinth after his conversion (1 Corinthians 1:26-29). It talked about those who had not been born of noble birth, those ordinary men and women that God wanted to use in extraordinary ways.

Between reading that Bible passage and the time that I lifted my face to see the audience, everyone's eyes had become as big as flying saucers, and I knew it was time. It was time to stop talking and take the next step. The harvest was ready. As I invited everyone who wanted to know Jesus to come forward, a flood of people rushed the stage. We backed up to make room for this enthusiastic crowd. One kid even bopped another one in the face while trying to get closer, and as I reached for the kid who had just been punched I spoke reassuringly to the other child and said, "God sees you." He stopped trying to push forward, folded his hands and was ready to pray. We all prayed together, and afterwards, I talked to them more and explained what being a church meant and that they could trust God.

After this people kept coming up to me offering thanks, saying they would never forget us. I acknowledged their gratitude but was drawn to the people still scattered throughout the rows of seats. These people had shrunk back. They were not ready to leave *or* move forward. They were just lost in thought and possibly moved by the show.

By this time I had felt an authority come over me that wasn't my own. The pain in my neck and the pressure on my chest was gone, and the Holy Spirit was there with us. We could feel it. It was thick, and it felt like love. As I looked out into the crowd I focused on an elderly Roma woman sitting alone and wearing a weathered and broken expression upon her face. I instructed my interpreter, "Follow me" as I walked over to this woman to share with her how special she is, and that God sees her, and that He loves her so much. She received my words and as they began to sink in and touch her heart she reached out and held my hand.

Eventually, the event wrapped up and the pain in my neck and the pressure on my chest came back. Throughout the drive back to our accommodations in Marghita, I gazed at the moon and was tossed and bounced in the back seat as the van was going through the winding bumpy roads. I was physically beat but feeling more alive than ever before: I came here with a limited understanding of the trials of poverty and wanted so much to figure out how I could help. Now I was confidently traveling through Transylvania after actually seeing God's power revive the poor and forgotten; and He did it through us, some friends with tattoos, and a simple street marionette theater—talk about loaves and fishes!

I heard those words that I had spoken to my interpreter, "Follow me" ring again and again in my head. I thought back to the other marionette production I had recently created for future tours, *Blessed are the Poor*, where I show Matthew, a tax collector, sitting at his tax booth and surrounded by everything he could ever want. Jesus just arrives and simply says, "Follow me."

As this new show was being crafted I often pondered, how did Jesus say those words? They seemed so direct and awkward in the Bible story. Did he suggest it casually, like it was just a good idea, or was it like a command? That night when I heard myself utter, "Follow me" to the interpreter, I felt an authority that wasn't my own and as I walked up to the Roma lady, I knew the interpreter would be there right behind me.

While continuing to bounce around in that van I began reflecting on the tour thus far, and it wasn't even done yet. I had seen crowds come forward to receive Jesus, lives being changed, wrongs made right, and sorrow turned to laughter—and I knew it was just a mere fraction of the power of God. Then I heard Him say to me, "See, do you still not understand? FOLLOW ME!" I couldn't resist that call and understood why Matthew didn't argue or even question it when Jesus said, "FOLLOW ME"–he just went. Matthew knew of the miracles Jesus was doing, and he knew what a privilege it was to follow Him. He would have been a fool not to. That night in the village of Popesti, I felt the tone of God's voice, and even though responding to it was hard, painful, and tiring, it was worth it. "Yes Jesus, I'll Follow!"

When I returned to Minneapolis that autumn I began writing a song and poem on my accordion to help me therapeutically process what I had experienced during these trials in Transylvania. The following is what I wrote:

I'll Follow

Verse 1

C min. - Cb Maj.
When I feel, I'm all alone...

Bb Maj. - F Maj cont.
I'll follow, I'll follow.

When I don't,know where to go...
I'll follow, I'll follow.
When darkness falls, all over me...
I'll follow, I'll follow.
Because you said, you'd never leave,
I'll follow, I'll follow.

Verse 2

When I am lost, and fear sets in,
I'll follow, I'll follow.
Even when my life looks grim,
I'll follow, I'll follow.
In this world, of pain and scorn
I'll follow, I'll follow.
Because you're knocking at my door,
I'll follow, I'll Follow...

Chorus

F min. - Db Maj. - Ab Maj. - Bb Maj.
My God

Verse 3

Because you died, and bore my shame,
I'll follow, I'll follow.
Because you rose, from the grave,
I'll follow, I'll follow.
Because you proved, your love to me,
I'll follow, I'll follow.
Now that I have been set free,
I'll follow, I'll follow.

Chorus

My God
Lord Jesus, we ask you to save us.
Lord Jesus, we want you to change us.

Verse 4

Here I am, now hear my praise,
I'll follow, I'll follow.
You changed the night, into day,
I'll follow, I'll follow.
You put the stars, all into place,
I'll follow, I'll follow.
You are my hope, my love and grace,
I'll follow, I'll follow.

Chorus

My God
My God
Lord Jesus, we ask you to save us.
Lord Jesus, we want you to change us.
Lord Jesus, we give you our praise.
Lord Jesus, we need you we pray.

I'll Follow YOUTUBE MUSIC VIDEO

In the winter of 2008 I recorded this song, and in 2010 I returned to Transylvania and performed *Blessed are the Poor* (a new Suitcase Sideshow production). After our performance in Borumlaca, the Roma children passionately sang for us in appreciation, the most haunting traditional song I had ever heard. Clearly they knew my love language. When we traveled to Cadea the second time, I wondered if a similar thing would happen again like the first, but it was different. In a heartbreaking turn of events I didn't get to see Samona. She had run away earlier that day and a search party was looking for her.

As we performed our new show the audience rocked back and forth in a heart wrenching display of self-soothing behavior. There were no hostile remarks passed between staff and residents. We reconnected with the man who had attended our first show and had initiated praying for the abusive caregivers. I was blessed to discover he had a picture of us in his room to remind him to pray. We also learned he was leading a Bible study for his friends and peers in the institution! We had been well remembered at the facility, as we were the only people to have ever brought marionettes and a theater to perform there.

Over the years I have seen many humanitarian servants struggle with a Messiah complex, and I am still not immune to it. We carry the weight of the world and feel it's all up to us to fix the world's injustices. It can be tempting to become easily impressed with the trials of the world, rather than God's power to redeem humanity. I have seen it ruin marriages, build unteachable pride, and totally suck people dry of their passion and joy. The moment we give into the lie that it's all up to us, is the moment we take on the belief that maybe we love the poor more than God does. But we are not heroes. Our systems are not heroes. We simply need to be there to serve Jesus Christ by serving them and do our part in the grand scheme of God's plan to restore a broken world.

MASKED WITH BEAUTY

TOLD BY PHILIP SHOREY

———•◆•———

(2007)

WE HAD JUST experienced some incredible acts of God and some intense trials in Romania. Now we were on the final stretch of the 2007 tour. We were supposed to return to Hungary, and do a soccer camp, but it got canceled, so we extended our time in Switzerland.

Switzerland is where cheese, chocolate, yodeling, and a history of peace prevail—so we anticipated a respite from the trauma we witnessed in Romania. We enjoyed taking a Sabbath day, visiting a chocolate factory, and even went to the circus. We easily fell in love with Switzerland, but amidst all the beauty and peace in the capital, Bern, we felt a heavy sadness and discord. On the surface it's covered in historic architecture, intoxicating chocolate, pure water from the mountains that you can drink from the decorative fountains throughout the city, and breathtaking views of the Alps—but we would learn that behind the mask of beauty were secluded neighborhoods housing legal drugs and prostitution.

The Kirchenfeldbrücke in Bern, Switzerland, is one of the tallest bridges in Europe. Its grand panoramic views of old town are breathtaking, but the locals shared the bridge's dark secret: there was a designated ambulance emergency parking spot at the bottom of the bridge, and jumping barriers due to the suicides that occur in its shadow. It's heartbreaking that in a society, sitting on top of the world's advancements, there is still so much despair. People need help. Our world needs help. We don't just need a better system; the best systems in the world will never save us. We need new hearts.

We were looking forward to being home soon, and yet we knew God had set this side of the tour up for a reason. We met with friends and discussed where we were going to perform the show. There were lots of suggestions but nothing was scheduled yet. There was bountiful entertainment competing for attention throughout the city, and lots of red tape—so pop-up toy theater was hard to arrange.

Then someone mentioned a place called *Reithalle*. It was the former site of old stables and a depot for stagecoaches. When the horses moved out, squatters moved in and it became a cultural multi-purpose center where drugs were centralized and legal. Here you could dine in a café, watch alternative films in the theater, easily find heroin, meth, or weed, and see creative stunts that the rest of the city prohibited. Despite all this perceived freedom, people were often robbed by needlepoint with the threat of HIV, and anything to do with God was forbidden. It was a risky place to bring my heirloom marionettes or the Gospel.

We entertained the idea of doing a show at *Reithalle*. We didn't want to just talk about how we were willing to bring the Gospel anywhere, but when it came down to it, run away. We sensed it was time to surrender our relationships, marionettes, and lives back to Jesus—again. We felt like Abraham offering our son Isaac up to God, not knowing what the outcome would be.

We were so scared to do this that we needed an extra ounce of confirmation about going forward with this show. I made some requests to God to affirm this was His will—similar to when Gideon put down fleeces to test God's answer to whether or not He really wanted Gideon to go into battle (Judges 6:33-40). I asked God for three things: a car so we didn't have to walk home and could make a quick exit if necessary, for more translators so we could talk to more people, and local people to participate with us in this effort. We needed the locals to be involved so we wouldn't just be flying in and out, but so the risk and investment was shared and taken seriously.

I already knew what this risk was like. I had put my reputation on the line in my own city. I knew it would be hard for our friends who use to hang out there to go back representing Jesus. After praying, we all trusted that God had brought us there. He provided a vehicle, translators, and local Christian believers.

When we arrived at dusk we could feel a sense of death everywhere. There were bright lights flooding the place, and crowds of people in little huddles cooking heroin with spoons over lighters. Andrew noticed one guy holding a heroin needle to his neck while using a broken rearview mirror to aim for a vein. The dealers were at the top of the stairs scoping out the premises. No one was in charge. Anything could happen at any moment and no one would be fazed.

We felt we should walk around and talk to people first. As I approached people sticking needles in their arms, the interpreter and I asked them the last thing on earth they probably expected to hear. "Do you mind if we perform a puppet show for you over there?" We talked with one guy while he cooked heroin, and I explained that we were on tour, and wanted his permission to do the show. He asked, "What's the show about?" I replied, "Hope." He exclaimed, "What!? You want to tell all of us junkies about hope?" I nodded in affirmation, but to be honest, I wasn't so sure that there could be hope in this place. Just looking around, all I could see were people that wanted to escape reality—but causing themselves more pain.

In a twist of humor, our request to perform a marionette show was lost in translation and some got the message that we wanted to perform a marijuana show. I thought that was funny—maybe God would use that to compel more people to see it.

Once I was able to get permission from almost everybody, it was time to set up. The general consensus regarding our request was, "Sure, do the show, I don't know if I'll watch it, but whatever..."

We found a spot where there weren't as many used needles scattered across the ground, we swept a few more out of the way, and set up the stage. I began to play my Singing Saw to set a calm atmosphere. I felt a slow and solemn melody flowing through my saw as I looked around. It was gaining some people's attention and a few people I had talked to came over to watch. When we were ready, I started with an introduction.

"This is a story about a murderer!" I said. "A bad man, one who was feared by many, but the story doesn't stop there, it is also a story about forgiveness, hope, and love!" Then I explained that this story changed my life, and I hoped it would change theirs. We cranked the volume so that those still doing drugs around the perimeter could hear the show. I couldn't imagine the trip they were about to face—a mix of creepy marionettes, drugs, and Jesus.

The show started out without any mishaps, but even though it was presented in German, I knew the flow of the story and waited for a glass bottle to be flung my direction at certain parts but it didn't. One friend even stood behind us, just to keep watch, but nothing happened.

There was only one moment when someone came charging towards us screaming "I DON'T BELIEVE IN THIS!" but about nine feet from the stage, he abruptly stopped and sat down to watch the rest of the show. We had prayed that God would keep the people at bay who would want to distract others from hearing the message, and He miraculously did.

Afterwards, I came out to explain the story in more depth, and offered the message of hope in Jesus. By the end of the night we had prayed with several people and our team had many good relationship forming conversations. We found that God had given us back our show and favor with the audience after we had put everything on the line.

For a long time before our show my interpreter had been prayerfully considering going into *Reithalle* to minister to the people there, and after we arrived in Bern, he felt affirmed in that prayer. He continued to visit and even began a ministry work. Over time, he partnered with the EMTs of an ambulance posted nearby and offered first aid. He was able to continue to freely share the love of Jesus, as well as meet their physical needs. His ministry grew and developed into a festival that we were later invited to.

Although there are places all over the world like Switzerland that wear a mask of beauty, only to cover up a deep human pain—I see it so honorable as an artist and messenger of the Gospel to serve God and serve my fellow man in peeling back those masks—so that true healing can take place. No risk can compare to those stories.

PHOTOS

Philip performs as a sailor

Philip and John-Mark as young puppeteers

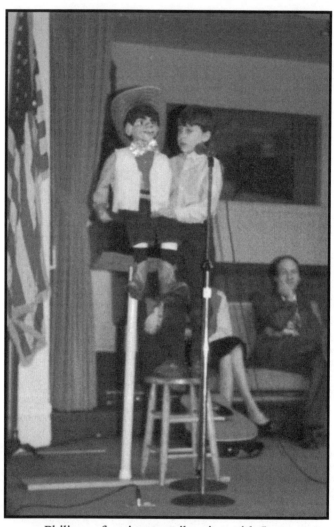
Philip performing ventriloquism with Scott

The Scallywaggin tour

The back of the Scallywaggin trailer

Creepy circus music

Madness of Folly production

Philip's prayer closet

Edgar and Marilyn pass on their marionettes to
Philip in Minneapolis

The 234 Brothel

Setting up under the bridge

Cadea

Philip with Andrew and Katie Dirks
at Bran Castle, Romania

Roma Village show

Reithalle, Bern Switzerland

GENERATION 5

>>>><<<<

AFTER WE FINISHED our tour in Switzerland, I sent a newsletter update to a handful of friends and incidentally selected a name I didn't recognize. This person must have signed up for my mailing list, so I didn't bother deselecting them because I figured they wouldn't mind.

The email read:

"Okay, things are coming to a close for us here in Europe. We leave for Berlin tomorrow and we will be connecting with NLM there and finishing up our tour. We have had a wonderful time here and in Switzerland things proved once again that God is our protector and our guide. We are forever changed by what happened in that county."

Much to my surprise, the next day, I received a reply from the unknown email recipient who said that she was in Berlin with friends, and that it would be grand to see my travelling show. I replied with the details about our show, which would be at 7pm the next day at Mauer Park behind a fence and a dirt road.

The following afternoon we learned our show had been cancelled, so we took the time to visit with friends who were participating in the No Longer Music (NLM) show in Berlin. The woman who had emailed me was also there, and in a shy manner, she worked up enough courage to introduce herself. She was gorgeous and looked very European. I didn't know where she was from—but I assumed Germany. She was nervous to talk to me, but luckily her friends had convinced her to introduce herself by saying, "It's not every day you see someone from your home city in a completely different country. Go talk to him—or we will!"

Her name was Sari (Sar-ē) Schwarzbauer and she recently started attending the very same Salvage Yard Church that I had been going to for years. She had just graduated from the University of Minnesota-Twin Cities and amazingly, she got on my mailing list after signing up during a church ministry fair that previous winter.

We started chatting and when Sari shared that she was starting a new job as a pediatric nurse once she got back to the states, I was shocked. A mentor of mine had recently made the offhand comment that I should marry a nurse. Maybe he was just kidding or maybe God spoke to me about it when he mentioned that, but here before me was a beautiful woman who was a nurse from my city and from my church! We both happened to travel across the world to meet in Berlin!

Sari was a little disappointed that I wouldn't be doing the show that day, but she and her friends stayed around the park to hang out. As she was watching No Longer Music set up for their concert, she felt Jesus asking her if she would ever sacrifice her career and lead a more unconventional life for Him. At that moment she said, "YES" and chose to surrender it to Him and experienced a 180-degree perspective change about what she would do with her life.

When we met in Berlin, something amazing was happening and I fell in love at first sight. We both agreed that when we returned home, we should hang out together. I always thought leaving puppets for soccer was going to be the best thing for me if I ever wanted to find a girlfriend—but just maybe it was the puppets after all that God was using to open a door into romance.

Upon returning home and attending the Salvage Yard Church, the following Tuesday, Sari approached me and said, "Hey, do you remember me?" I replied, "Of course!" and after a little talking, I asked her if she wanted to see the community house where I lived with a bunch of other guys. She agreed to the plan and even had a bike rack on her car, so she was conveniently able to bring my bike home for me. Together we drove to the Oakland Hotel. I knew my life wasn't very ordinary and would possibly even scare her away, but if we were going to be friends I didn't want to pretend I was someone I wasn't. Although, now I know that she immediately figured I was a little different by the way I smelled in Germany and that she was open to adventure that Tuesday night in South Minneapolis. We bought a Hot-N-Ready pizza from Little Caesars and shared it on the back porch with some of my housemates while listening to gunshots being fired off nearby like fireworks. But even that didn't seem to scare her away, so I asked if we could hang out again and she agreed.

I never let a date finish without planning when Sari and I would see each other again. This woman was blowing away all my "ideal wife" expectations! God knew that I wanted the right lady who would fit my calling and push me closer to Him. She was from a good family, she clearly heard God's voice, she had a good sense of humor and style, she was a total natural with marionettes (similar to Fern whom Alex had fallen in love with), very wise and kind hearted, and she reminded me of Arwen from *The Lord of the Rings.* This was perfect because secretly I always saw myself as Aragorn --so we were even a match made in "Middle-Earth."

On top of all that, as we later conversed about our family heritage, I learned that her ancestors were from Karlstad, Sweden, and had also planned to voyage to North America aboard the *Titanic* on April 10, 1912. Her great-grandfather Otto Olofsson-Gustafson, his uncle Lars, and brother John, were hired to work in exchange for their fare across the Atlantic in the boiler room of the *Titanic*; however, all three men missed the ship's departure because they were enjoying a farewell visit in a local pub with some friends and lost track of time; although it was rumored that Otto never took a sip.

I can see it now, like another blockbuster *Titanic* film; my family, the Rasmussen's, parading away from the docks of South Hampton, heads held high and following Marie (possibly played by Nicole Kidman due to her characterized strong-will) with her conviction to exchange their tickets for a different passage to the new land; when around the corner—with panic in their eyes—comes three men who run past them, out of breath, and moments too late as the gangway is retracted from the dock. They had missed their ship and (in a swell of Celine Dion's *My Heart Will Go On*) they kick cleats, throw their hats, and curse the wind. Otto sulks and solemnly follows the Rasmussen's trail to the White Star and Cunard ticket offices, hoping for another chance across the great Atlantic.

It's fun to imagine our families spending some time together on the shore of South Hampton. Maybe they became good friends or got into some kind of brawl over a poker game in a pub and swore to never to see each other again. Possibly that is why Otto boarded the *RMS Laconia* to Boston on June 11, 1912, instead of the *SS Laurentic* with the Rasmussen's to Quebec City.

We will probably never know for sure, but one thing we do know is that direct descendants of those two families had to return across the Atlantic to meet in Berlin on the warm evening of August 24, 2007 almost 100 years later. This meeting between us may not have ever occurred if our ancestors had boarded the *Titanic*, a mighty but ill-fated passenger liner, which sank April 15, 1912 after hitting an iceberg.

Sari and I married on May 30, 2009. We spent our first year focusing together on seeking God's will for our calling before we set off to Europe on our first tour with a *family* traveling act, The Suitcase Sideshow. One of the goals for this tour was to transition The Suitcase Sideshow from "my thing" to "our thing."

In my early years of missions, people were always giving me the same advice: "You travel a lot and you should while you're young and single. Do it while you can before you get married." Then I became married, but as Sari and I continued to travel and do missions abroad the remarks were similar: "Oh, you should travel now while you don't have any kids or a house." Other people would tell us, "Wow, I wish I could do that kind of thing." Secretly we would think, "You can!" You can forfeit the "American dream" and replace it with God's dream, which is way bigger than anyone can imagine. Whether it appears mundane or adventurous, you too can live a life of sacrifice in obedience to what God is calling you to do."

Then, by a crazy miracle, we were able to buy a duplex in Northeast Minneapolis, and it released us to keep answering the call even more. Then people would continue to say, "Do it before you have kids."

At the time this book is being compiled, three members of Generation 5 have already been born! Sari and I are parents of two sons: Axel Vincent Shorey and Casper Robin Shorey, and another strong-willed and determined girl in the family, Juneau Celeste Shorey. All of our children have traveled with us on multiple occasions. As long as God allows us to continue to serve Him in this way, we will keep taking bold steps of faith and obedience. We will not conform to worshiping comfort. As our family grows, the calling stays the same, but the method will adjust to how we live it out.

Each phase of life doesn't change our calling, it just requires more faith. So we think that instead of encouraging young people to, "Do it now before you have kids/house/spouse," we should encourage others to follow their calling by saying "Do it now, so the faith you build early on will be a stepping stone to building more faith as life gets more complicated." But God is good, and it's my prayer that the legacy and impact that these stories have on our kids will establish them in a heritage of service to Jesus Christ and the poor in spirit.

Our children have a valuable part in our ministry; they are not just tagalongs. This perspective stems from the way my parents raised me to participate in traveling ministry and what my parents learned from their parents!

When we are overseas fulfilling missions work as a family, it gets hard. We believe that we *all* work together as a family unit in God's calling. The family isn't meant to revolve around the kids, which can turn them into a false idol, it is meant to revolve around Jesus and the kids are a valuable part of that. We hope they will continue to be part of the family calling until God gives them their own particular callings. They are important—and we have seen walls and barriers broken simply because we have a baby or kids with us. Families relate to us like never before and will listen to our message and watch our show. God is good and has always provided for us, but still, it's never easy.

Each generation and model of ministry must discover how to accommodate children and include them at an early age. When I was growing up, I traveled with my family in a camper, learned puppets, and helped count the offerings after services to make it more fun. My parents had me sing, hold a prop, or operate a puppet from a very young age. We performed in churches, and it was a safe place to have family events and kids ministry; however, I sometimes perform in squats, homeless shelters, and prisons—where kids may not be safe or welcomed. We travel overseas, and don't have a camper to call home, so we run the risk of having young kids wreck someone else's home. These are real risks. Risks of exposing your kids to something they are not ready for, risks of ruining a mission relationship because your kids acted out and messed up their house. Risks of being judged as parents from new cultural norms. But following Jesus isn't supposed to be safe! It's revolutionary! Maybe it's marching in a pagan parade with your son, singing "Amazing Grace." Maybe it's preaching to street kids in Mexico using your kids as an illustration for their Heavenly Father's love. Maybe it's handing them a squirt gun during a storm scene for them to completely take their part too far. Maybe it's being on tour and watching your son softly yet boldly tell a cynical old man that Covid-19 wasn't God's fault, but Satan's, because Satan hates God's creation.

The enemy knows where we are the weakest—and parenting is one of the most vulnerable things you will ever do. Traveling as a family means having to navigate bedtime, discipline, and trying to be culturally sensitive with kids who are not culturally aware. It involves having to manage different foods, and changes in time-zones, which can feel like having to go through a child's infancy all over again. It means having to balance how other cultures parent, even when it contrasts how we choose to parent. The called family has to be willing to be flexible with celebrations like birthdays and anniversaries. For us it also means sacrificing lazy days of summer in Minnesota, which for Minnesota residents, is probably the only reason anyone in their right mind would actually live in this climate.

Often times we work with people who don't have kids, and don't understand kid schedules, but we strive to be accommodating and hospitable and to remember that other people have not necessarily bought into our radical parenting philosophy. It might be easier to choose to live some kind of Christian version of the American dream—where you play it safe and pursue worldly success and security, but it is more beneficial to the children to live a life that requires faith. Together, we have seen prayers answered, and shown them first-hand the hurt in the world and how the message of Jesus can heal the world. We have had to become creative in how we chose to involve them at each stage of their development. It may be the most impactful way they will see church as alive and applicable and not an archaic museum. Alone, I may travel faster, but together, we will all go farther.

I am excited to see what God will do with my kids as they grow up, and even though I come from a family of missionaries that has used puppets for several generations, I won't mind if their lives don't include puppets at all. My prayer is simply for each of them to have God's best in their lives and that He reveals Himself to them in ways that they can understand. I pray that my kids will share Christ's love with the next generation that follows, just as my parents did with me, and those who served before them.

Generation 5 is based on the memories, journaling, emails, and newsletters of Philip and Sari J. Shorey.

I'M NO TOURIST

TOLD BY PHILIP SHOREY

———◆———

(2002 - 2010)

I HEARD ABOUT an art festival in Lubiąż, Poland, that takes place on the grounds of an old castle. Attendees would gather there to share their creative skills, and while creating art they would encourage one another in spiritual ways. The festival is unlike anything held in the world, and it began as a reunion for the artistic and free-spirited people who gave their lives to Jesus at a No Longer Music concert under the Iron Curtain of Communism.

The following year I became intrigued by the idea of visiting Poland and this festival because of the origin stories shared by my friends in NLM. In the 1980s, they were banned by government officials from playing at a punk rock festival because they were seen as a "Western" threat; however, the Polish government did not have jurisdiction on church property, so a Catholic Church allowed the band to play on their front steps. God moved powerfully over everyone, and one year later as the movement grew into an amazing gathering full of people from all walks of life, it became known as SLOT Art Festival.[m]

In 2003, while backpacking through Europe for the first time and set on attending SLOT Art Festival, I met a punk rocker while riding an overnight train from Berlin to Poland.

He was hopping the train illegally and we communicated using a mix of charades and broken English. We shared in our mutual heritage that we each had grandfathers (mine on my dad's side) who had fought in World War II, over the land we were passing through. He told me about Nazi skinheads, and then showed me scars all over his body saying Nazi skinheads had made them. He made it sound like everyone in Wrocław (which was the town where I needed to transfer trains) was a skinhead, and since I was wearing combat boots and clothes with holes in them; somehow I fit the bill of a punk rocker and was asking for a beating. He warned me, "Skinheads hate punks." I was scared out of my mind.

When I arrived in Wrocław around 3AM, everyone was a suspect. I hid behind a shed near Wrocław Główny until the sun came up hoping a skinhead wouldn't discover me. In the morning under the light of the sun, things looked a little bit more optimistic and less dramatic. I didn't know where to go to catch my next train and I thought I'd maybe try hitchhiking, but then while eating street vendor food on the station steps, someone approached me and asked in English if I was going to SLOT. When I answered affirmatively, she kindly gave me directions and told me which train to take.

My next transfer was to a bus in Wołow that would take me to the festival. Once I arrived in Wołow, I was desperate to use the toilet, which ended up just being a ditch in the dirt around the edge of a shack. The dead rodents floating in the excrement continued to reinforce my intense impression of Poland and tone for survival. Had I turned back or perseverated on these first impressions, I would have missed out on some of the greatest beauty imaginable—when I entered the festival grounds I was dumbstruck. SLOT Art Festival took place on the ruins of Cistercian Abbey of Lubiąż, which dates back to the 1100s. It took centuries to build and is the largest Cistercian Abbey in the world. It was a masterpiece!

There was so much going on, and so much to explore that one could easily lose themselves in their imagination and truly believe they were living on the set of an *Indiana Jones* adventure. Every turn you took through the vast halls and courtyards of the Abby, you might stumble upon a rave, a fire spinning show, or a workshop of Polish women practicing some kind of enchanting folk vocal technics. Much of the castle hadn't been gated off yet, and you could literally walk up to the balconies through the rafters to the base of the two towers. I attended workshops in the high-ceiling ballrooms of a castle, saw art exhibits in a grand but dilapidated cathedral, and attended concerts in a once lavish courtyard. On one occasion, I was given a tour into the bowels of the cathedral where crypts of the Silesian dukes and the artists who crafted and sculpted the mosaics and statues of this world heritage site were buried. Sadly, during the Second World War, Nazis gathered some of the coffins to one spot, and destroyed the rest to use the grounds and the catacombs as secret research labs and manufacturing plants.

I overcame my initial fright and fell in love with Poland and everything that was Polish. It is a beautiful country, with beautiful people and beautiful culture. Every time I visit, it becomes harder and harder to leave. I appreciate how the people are so hospitable, and that they are so supportive when we attempt to speak their language, which was oppressed for many years. I love their zeal, which kept them so spirited and vibrant despite the oppression of communism. God has given us so many gifts through touring Poland: lifelong friendships, courage, and possibly even a "guardian angel" whom I met while attending SLOT in 2007.

I was traveling with Andrew and Katie by train across Poland, and we were frequently being asked if we had been robbed yet. We even met a couple of backpackers with beaten up faces franticly asking if we could help them because they had just been robbed on a train. I felt a chill go down my spine as I knew that Satan was trying to scare me saying, "What are you doing, bringing your friends into a trap with all your heirloom marionettes only to get stolen and beaten up? Is this really worth it?" My friend Katie asked me, "Do you think we should go wait over there instead?" In a frenzy of emotions I just responded with, "No," while thinking... "I will NOT give into this fear, I will not be afraid. *Greater is He who is in me than he who is in the world!* We will wait here like we are supposed to and be just fine." We were just fine, and have never been robbed in Poland.

When we arrived in Lubiąż we found that our accommodations were at a mental hospital. Every night we could hear groaning and screaming, which was unsettling and made sleep come slowly. I couldn't stop thinking that I was lost in a poem by Tom Waits, and I wondered if my dreams were going to resemble *The Raven* by Edgar Allen Poe "...nevermore."

In the morning, we woke up to find a stray black dog contentedly sleeping on my shoes. She stayed in my shadow everywhere I went for that whole week at SLOT Art Festival, and only left my side around dinnertime to dig in the trashcans and beg from other people. Then she always found her way back to the mental hospital and waited up for me in the morning.

I named her Patches. She would sneak into different workshops with me, would come when I called her in Polish, stay when I told her to stay, and if a girl sat too close to me, she would wiggle in between us. Perhaps this little stray dog was my guardian angel, keeping Polish women at bay. Patches' ways were certainly angelic, and she certainly captured and guarded my heart in an otherwise temptingly romantic atmosphere weeks before I met Sari.

It was also in Poland that our street performing skills with The Suitcase Sideshow became fine-tuned, and we experienced a rhythm of closing our show and seeing people coming to Jesus in the streets. We began to expect it and had faith to believe that it would happen again and again. People have even found me years later and told me they prayed with me after our show and they are still following Jesus; in addition to those immediate responses I also received emails from people saying they didn't have the courage to stand and pray with us, but they wanted to and our show changed their lives. Poland was ripe for the harvest. Their eagerness for truth and hope was helping many people find Jesus in an intimate and unreligious way.

I have collectively spent years in Poland touring with different groups and shows. One time I was touring for a couple of months in 2010 with our friends Noah and Wendy, and about two weeks into a Polish Tour, we had already seen God do some radical things. The Suitcase Sideshow had performed in juvenile jails, public schools, street corners, and plazas. The shows were just getting better and better. Then we were told our next show would be in an amphitheater that could hold about 3,000 people in a major tourist destination on an island in the Baltic Sea. I chuckled a little when I heard that because I thought the organizer was joking. When I realized that he wasn't I kept my comments to myself until I saw the place.

When we arrived on the island, I looked at the outdoor amphitheater, and then I looked at our stage that had gone ahead of us to be set up. I could no longer contain my laughter about the absurdity of the situation. I said, "Our stage is so miniscule compared to this place. Why would people come to see our performance? We are barely visible from the back." I scoped out the area nearby and identified a prime performance location in a park right next to the amphitheater. There I saw many young people casually lounging around and I suggested, "We should do our show over there, by the people. We should go to the people! They won't even know anything is going on in here because you can't even see our stage from where you walk in." But then my tour organizer shared with me that he had gone through great lengths to receive permission from the mayor to use this space. This organizer had not steered us wrong yet, so I reluctantly complied, "We'll give it a chance."

Sari, Noah, and I started playing some music on the accordion, clarinet, and the Singing Saw when a few people curiously wandered into the amphitheater. I wasn't initially impressed, but the more we played the more people wandered in. I conceded, "Okay, maybe we will have a little bit of a crowd here. We should do our show before we lose it."

When we perform our show in open spaces like parks and streets, it's typical for people to watch for a bit then depart before it is over. The show we did on that tour was twenty-five minutes and we understand that typically people's attention span and available time may not last the entire duration of the performance; however, this was not the case in the amphitheater. People just kept coming and coming, and nobody was leaving. As more people kept pouring in to hear our modern stories about Jesus and what it would be like if Christ came to Poland today, I intermittently peeked over the curtains and I was shocked! I repented and said to God, "I'm sorry. If you are doing something here, I want to be part of it."

When the show was over, I figured God was performing a miracle, so I gave a full Gospel message and asked if anyone wanted to know Jesus in this way—to kneel with me right there on the concrete of the amphitheater. A bunch of people knelt down with me to pray and receive Jesus!

I was further awestruck because most of the audience was tourists, taking a break from life. Tourists generally want easygoing entertainment that helps them forget about the hardships they faced—and that was certainly not the message we were offering. It would have been easy to give into the spiritual lies that said, "You are doing them a disservice by being here. Stop it right now!" But we weren't doing them a disservice at all. This vacation could end up being a vacation that they would never forget if we pressed forward. It could give fresh perspective and hope to their lives, and could even be the way God reaches more of Poland when those tourists return home.

The local church had Bibles to hand out and was able to get contacts from the people in order to follow up. This included a nine-year-old boy who came up to me and said, "I have been going to a school where I have heard about Jesus all my life, but I have never wanted to follow Him until right now."

That particular show reminded me that with God all things are possible. He had put us there against all mission philosophies and methods that we had seen work in other places and He did something radical with, what at first glance, seemed foolish. His ways are *always* better than our ways.

Upon leaving northern Poland by way of rickety trains, we reconvened with more amazing comrades to perform shows in another unconventional tourist destination. I was introduced to the wonderful Filip and Agnieszka during my first visit to SLOT. At that time they shared stories about another festival that God had placed on their hearts and invited me to join them. It was called Polish Woodstock and is the biggest open-air festival in Europe with over 500,000 people attending annually. Midway through a six month Suitcase Sideshow tour in 2010, we finally went to that festival with them.

Matthew 7:13&14 reads "...for the gate is wide and the way is broad that leads to destruction, and there are many who enter through it. For the gate is small and the way is narrow that leads to life, and there are few who find it." As messengers of the Gospel, our purpose is to go to the people who are on the broad road, rescue as many of them as we can, warn them of the dangers ahead, and help them find the road that leads to life. This was our hope and we strove to do it wisely.

Let me tell you what the 'broad road that leads to destruction' looks like.

Sari and I arrived at the festival two days early with additional friends from Steiger and the SLOT Art Festival. After we set up our initial camp, we were warned that an undetonated warhead from World War II had been found where a latrine was being dug. We were evacuated and had to relocate the camp. The situation was very eye-opening of the impact of an old war that still effects life today, yet humorous, in a bizarre sort of way, because we were Woodstock refugees being forced to relocate our camp somewhere else.

Then we began setting up our tents within the Boanerges Motorcycle Club campsite. This is a Christian motorcycle club that hosts a bike rally during Woodstock and serves bikers by keeping their bikes safe during the festival. They also serve a meal each day and host a café marquee where they provide entertainment throughout the week. They considered our group to be their guests, and it was a blessing because each day we were sent out into the thick of the festival with a covering of prayer from these fellow brothers and sisters.

The heat was intense. There was a perpetual dust cloud hovering over the entire festival grounds, and at every turn we discovered intoxicated teenagers passed out on the ground. Sari always paused to make sure these listless people were still breathing and turned to a recovery position so if they vomited they wouldn't drown. Every few minutes we would see four-wheelers from the festival pulling a trailer with an unconscious person strapped to it. Fully naked guys and girls staggered around the festival like zombies and fights occasionally broke out.

After a few days of hot weather the whole place reeked of urine. We estimated that the port-a-potty ratio was maybe less than 1 for every 1,000 people. One afternoon, I had a great talk with a friend—but discovered that we had spent the past three hours sitting where nearby campers had designated their outdoor toilet. That explained why it had been the only shady and quiet spot we could find!

The main organizer of the festival is involved in Hare Krishna, and throughout the festival there is constant Hare Krishna music and mantras with elaborate parades of devotees following their idol in a huge wagon. The Hare Krishnas serve free food which has been sacrificed to their idol and provide meditations and astrology readings in their tents.

Also present and active at this festival are about 500 priests, nuns, and monks who walk around talking with people about Jesus and reminding people to perform their own sacraments. Some of them wore clown wigs to be relevant to the party scene and were very charismatic. They provided a network to evacuate the kids who are being broken and abused by the environment around them. The festival is deceptively presented on the official website as family friendly and a wholesome reward for youth who raised money for charity, but once you get there, you learn otherwise. It's like the scene from Pinocchio where boys go to Pleasure Island—but are punished by their desires and turn into donkeys.

Most of the kids we met hated religion and loved this festival because they were trying to escape structured life and looking for freedom. While eating lunch one day, I conversed with a few teens about their experience at the festival. "This place is great, you can do whatever you want and nobody cares." As I heard this, I saw a four-wheeler ambulance carrying another unconscious person out of the festival strapped to a trailer. I grieved internally and thought, "This isn't a music festival, this is where kids go to die!"

This experience further revealed to me how errant the American perspective is regarding Europeans and alcohol. We have frequently heard the claims that "Europeans don't drink to get drunk" and "they can hold their alcohol because they start drinking at such an early age." But in reality, they are no more immune to the potentially ill effects of alcohol than other nations.

We performed our marionette show seven times, and our first five performances were held on the main path located between the vendors and the Hare Krishna village. People's attention span at Woodstock only lasts a few minutes and looking back on it now, the atmosphere at Polish Woodstock when we presented our shows was very similar to trying to perform at Mardi Gras in New Orleans years later. It was quite challenging trying to present a slightly contemplative show in the French Quarter when everything around you is also screaming for your attention.

The surprising bright moment at Mardi Gras was our one-year-old Juneau who stole the show as the youngest attendee of Mardi Gras and drew people to talk and pray with us. She was completely unfazed by the party atmosphere, until a giant demon on stilts tried to make her laugh and give her light-up beads. She screamed in terror. I held her tight as she nuzzled into my neck and whispered in her ear, "Papa is here and Jesus is stronger."

So, we weren't surprised during the Woodstock shows that we would lose some people, but because our show, at the time, consisted of short scenes the people that wandered off would always be replaced with a new crowd walking by. After each performance, my friend Filip or I, would preach. We did the show in both Polish and German and saw an acceptance of Christ, while others just wanted to know more. It was great and opened up more opportunities to share how much Jesus loved everyone there! In such a place full of deceit, we were joyfully blasting the truth of God in a way never heard before. We were planting seeds to change people's worldview of Jesus. Filip would preach "We're not here to tell you about religion, but to offer you a relationship with God!" And I would add, "Jesus is more powerful than other gurus and idols because He didn't just talk about love, He proved His love for you on the cross!"

Sometimes we would just stop the show and start preaching over the massive confusion of the festival. For me, there is very little that compares to the thrill of sharing the Gospel in life and death situations with fellow comrades when we are surrounded by chaos. I imagine it is like Pastor John Harper who had the foresight in telling people on the *Titanic* while it was going down, "Get off the ship, it's sinking! Believe in the Lord Jesus Christ and you will be saved!"[n]

The sixth show we did was for a group of 100 bikers in the Boanerges' Motorcycle café in the camp where we were staying. Before our show, they were rocking out and dancing to a favorite local band. Encore after encore they returned to play more music and the crowd didn't want them to stop; but after seven encores the stage managers insisted it was our turn. How do you follow that crowd-pleasing act with a puppet show for a bunch of hardcore bikers? As we went on stage the crowd booed and hissed while the stage managers feared they had just made a big mistake and thrown us into the lion's den. There was nothing about my family's experience in marionette ministry that could have prepared me for this moment.

We began by playing a song on the accordion and Singing Saw. Three people unenthusiastically clapped and the rest continued booing and were outraged that a puppet show had taken the place of their favorite band. I then told them who we were, what the show was about, and that we were going to do a hardcore puppet show for them. They remained unimpressed.

Amidst the cackling and mocking we cut our musical set short and just began doing the show. Sari was trembling, and I just tried to assure her that it would be okay (despite my own uncertainty), but by the end of the first scene the whole café was completely hushed. It was as if we had been fed to the lions, but just like Daniel, the lions' jaws were shut and for 25 minutes, we had a captivated audience of rough bikers totally enthralled by our puppet show. We actually shared the Gospel to a bunch of bikers using puppets!

Afterwards I preached the Gospel and shared, "Jesus is not weak, but strong." I continued to challenge their common cultural notion that Christ is delicate and said, "If someone took a bullet for you, would you call them weak, or strong? I would call them my best friend and the strongest most loving friend in the world! Especially if He came back from the dead! That's Jesus!" Later I had the opportunity to lead one audience member to Jesus and prayed with others.

Another awe-striking part was witnessing the atmosphere of the audience altered after the show. People remained in the café and sat quietly and calmly in reflection. Without a doubt many people were processing what they had just witnessed. One of the leaders of the Boanerges Christian motorcycle club told me he had been reaching out to this scene for many years and had never seen these tough guys so enraptured by a demonstration so direct about Jesus. He encouraged me, "You need to keep doing this in Poland. There is an open window here for you, and God is using what you are doing."

God has used Poland to be such a blessing to me. There is much about it that holds a deep place in my heart. Performing in Poland's Roma villages, schools, orphanages, prisons, street corners, and festivals has no doubt shaped who I am and what I love. Later, we even realized through DNA testing, that my wife is quite Polish; a pleasant surprise for both of us. I have spent many years there intermittently touring with The Suitcase Sideshow, speaking, doing workshops, and even developing new models of evangelism with silent film and orchestral methods. Some people have mentioned they think I have a Slovak soul—but for me, when you find a place that connects to your creative and spiritual interests and works for what you do, you just keep going back. I'm thankful it was Poland.

Our final Polish Woodstock show took place on the second largest stage in the festival. We were given ten minutes to perform, so we did an abridged version of the show and followed it with a condensed message. We couldn't do much more but plant seeds and continue to just blast love and the name of Jesus into the festival; however, the stage manager really enjoyed it and requested we come back year after year to perform more. Maybe someday we will have an opportunity to return, but for now we continue to pray as every year more of our friends go to be a light where so many kids go to die.

W A R -
STRICKEN
L A N D S

TOLD BY PHILIP SHOREY

———•◆•———

(2010 - 2015)

WE HAVE RECEIVED more requests to come to Ukraine than anywhere else, and on one of our tours through Poland we kept encountering Ukrainians who thought our show would do really well in their country. Since that time I have made three trips to Ukraine. The first one inspired us to bring our show. The second one prepared us to bring our show, and the third one was to perform and tour with our show. It was a long process that began many years before the first visit or encounters with so many encouraging Ukrainians. There had been a shared sense between Sari, myself, and our friend Filip that God was calling us to go further east. We needed to respond.

In 2010 we toured extensively throughout the Schengen Area of Europe and needed to leave and return for our visa waiver to reset. We were invited to carpool in a quick boarder hop from Poland to Ukraine and back. Because of our presence in the vehicle, the driver and his wife were able to double their returning allowance of gas, cigarettes, and vodka— which were much cheaper to purchase in Ukraine than in Poland.

While in Ukraine, we drove up on a wedge to tilt the car as they pumped gas so the tank would fill it to the very top. We visited grocery stores with no advertisings, and the only markings on packages were their contents. I understood this to be remnant of their communist background. If you wanted rice, there is a generic bag of rice. Then we spent about six hours in border purgatory waiting to return to Poland and endured a lot of questioning. I remember being on a bridge straddling the two countries at 4am and listening to Bonnie Tyler on the local radio sing *Holding Out for a Hero* and thinking, "Yeah that's me. I need that song right now."

After that introductory visit, we were pumped and made a connection with some Ukrainians who wanted to help us translate the show, but for some reason, it didn't work out. Then another year, while teaching at the Steiger School in Germany, we met several Ukrainians. We performed The Suitcase Sideshow and it felt like a divine opportunity to collaborate with them. But again, nothing came to fruition. I began to wonder if this was something I wanted, or if it was actually from God. Then finally, we were connected with someone through Steiger who was willing to take a leap of faith with us and organize the translation of the show into Russian.

In 2013, we journeyed to Ukraine for the second time. This time our agenda was to record the show into Russian. We were doing our first tour with a baby and had just come from the Czech Republic. Our infant son Axel was a traveling miracle. He loved being held, and on tour, that's exactly what he got. We have lovely friends in Prague, who were a pleasure to work with, and had provided a European base before flying to Ukraine and in and out of Europe. We landed in Kiev, thinking, "Yes, we have arrived in Ukraine"—only to discover that we still had a five hour drive east through bumpy roads with a kind man who didn't know any English. We leaned into the knowledge that God had brought us here, and how it was His calling on us to go further east. We continued on our journey, knowing that we might have postponed this trip if we were aware that we were going to have to drive a four-month old baby five hours through an unkempt highway in Ukraine after our long flight. We were totally in God's hands and miraculously Axel slept most of the way.

About halfway though, we took a break at a truck stop, and I noticed a bunch of ladies dressed as if they were going clubbing. Later I asked our host, if there was a nightclub around there. When my friend told me there wasn't, I knew exactly what had been going on. I had seen the same thing in Romania and Brazil, and the very thought breaks my heart every time. Ladies in small towns sometimes prostitute themselves out to truck drivers and other travelers, or they work for pimps and are kidnapped foreigners. I remembered seeing this in Romania, and it had such an impact on me that when I returned home (and still to this day) whenever I see college girls, dressed to impress, walking down the sidewalk late at night in Dinkytown on the University of Minnesota's campus, my first reaction is a flashback to that night and I feel terrified for those girls.

Returning home from the mission field can feel like Rambo returning home in *First Blood*. "You just don't turn it off." *Missionary* PTSD (post-traumatic stress disorder) is a real thing. Traveling changes a person, as it should.

Over the following week, we finalized the Russian translation of our show and had it recorded into Russian by talented members of a church in Sumy, Ukraine. We finally had a completed show for the Russian-speaking world, and we had a great time getting it. We fell in love with Ukraine and the people of Ukraine, and we were so excited to return.

In the following year of 2014 the Ukrainian Revolution happened, and then war broke out on the border of Russia and the Crimean Peninsula. That was also the year my son Casper was born, and it wasn't feasible to plan a summer tour because of his August due date—let alone a tour through war stricken lands. We had a heart for the people in this war-torn country, and kept up-to-date on the local events. We sent funds to aid our friends as they ministered to soldiers and provided them with MP3 players uploaded with an audible bible.

The war continued with no end in sight, and the following year I knew that I had made a promise and it was time to tour The Suitcase Sideshow in Ukraine– no matter the situation. It was time to trust God and not give in to fear. Based on how I had seen some people respond to the show in Poland, who had fought in a war, I pondered if this might actually be a beautiful time for God to work in the brokenness and show us all His power to bring about healing.

Once in a Roma village in Poland, I was preaching about forgiveness after our show and a man interrupted me from the back and yelled, "What about me? Can God love a killer? I saw them die in the war." Knowing nothing about his life story, all I could speak was the truth. "Yes he can, just like Paul who killed many Christians, but God adored him and used him to write much of the Bible" I shouted back, and saw locals comfort and minister to the gentleman. I later learned that this man had killed and was traumatized by it. Every night he would drown his sorrow in alcohol. He was deeply touched by these words, but when I went to find him after the show I learned that since it was twilight he was already actively intoxicating himself in anticipation of his nightly torments.

Because of the instability in Ukraine, we felt it wasn't wise for us to bring our children at this time. God provided me with a friend (Sam Erickson) to tour with and, for the first time since being married, I toured without my family. I didn't want to leave my family and head into an unpredictable situation, but we all knew it was the right choice. I parted ways with Sari, Axel and Casper, who went to stay with friends in Bulgaria before meeting up with me in Moscow for the next half of the tour.

As I returned to Ukraine for the third time. We performed the first show for the local church; we would be working around Sumy (15 minutes from Russia and 700km from the fighting). It was their first time seeing the finalized Russian language production, and afterwards there was a light-bulb moment for our host regarding its potential impact. Finally, we were ready. We talked about where it would be most effective and then decided on the town square. But the next day rain sent us to a shopping mall.

I'm always reluctant to perform in malls, but my friends were insistent that the owner of the mall was fully open to a marionette show with "Christian values." So rather than not doing the show at all, I conceded and God led us to perform next to an ATM. My favorite parts in that performance were the references to money and materialism, which were ironically being made in a mall, the modern day temple to the cultural materialistic gods—a dramatic swing from their communist past. A number of people watched segments of the show, but due to all the mall distractions it was hard to keep the crowd; however, one man missed most of the show but came up after hearing the preaching. He wanted a Bible and came to church the following Sunday.

Our next two shows were outside on the town square and next to a river. This was where we were a little more comfortable and in our element. God had been doing some radical things through our show in Poland that summer, and before arriving, I knew He wanted to continue that momentum here at our first open air show in Ukraine. We maintained a crowd of approximately thirty people and after the show I gave a Gospel message. Then I asked people to kneel with me to receive Jesus right there if they wanted to know the kind of Jesus I was talking about. Kneeling on uncovered public ground is a pretty big stretch for most people, and culturally this is one of the most humbling things a Ukrainian can do—but many people did! Bibles were handed out and contact information was exchanged with the local church. This included a woman and her two children who accepted Jesus into their lives right there in the square. She appreciated the bold message because her husband had recently died of a drug overdose.

No Longer Music would also be coming to Sumy in a couple of weeks, so we all felt we should prepare the way and visit small towns to gather people for their visit—a kind of preparatory "John the Baptist Tour." Villagers couldn't believe we would come to them instead of the great city of Kiev. Many towns had never had a public display of the Gospel, and many people had never seen a puppet show before.

Everywhere we went people prayed with us to receive Jesus, and gave their contact information to the local church. In some towns the local church was just a few women and now they had many families that were interested in a relationship with Jesus! In another town, a bunch of teens came from an English class, got connected to the church, and were bused to the No Longer Music show in Sumy a couple weeks later.

In that same town, a woman approached me afterwards and said, "I need Jesus." She had just received notice of her son being drafted to go to war. After our show, she was introduced to a woman from the church who committed to meet with her regularly, pray for her and her son, and read the Bible together as they went through that challenging time. She had tears in her eyes as we prayed with her. Jesus was healing brokenness in Ukraine. The church was growing and people received hope at a time when it seemed that all hope was lost.

After that show we also met and prayed with someone who inquired about my job back home, and I told her that I taught piano lessons. I became shocked and thrilled when she told me that the actual piano Tchaikovsky used to compose his music was nearby and that we could visit it!

We had already seen the statues of Frédéric Chopin and Johann Sebastian Bach on this tour. Watching Axel climb on the Frédéric Chopin statue and see the resting place of his heart in Warsaw was a dream come true for me. I had dreamed about seeing another historic marker of Pyotr Tchaikovsky or Igor Stravinsky in Ukraine—but I could never have envisioned such a blessing as viewing this part of history.

On the way back home, we found the museum which was in

the vacation home where Tchaikovsky wrote much of the music we hear at Christmas time. The museum was closed, but by some miracle the night watchman opened the door. He looked just like Barbosa from *Pirates of the Caribbean,* and had two rows of gold teeth and offered to give us a private tour.

My jaw dropped when I saw the beautiful white grand piano alone in the room that wielded the *Nutcracker Sweet* to come alive. I timidly approached the piano while the old floor creaked beneath my feet. It was like I was in the presence of a king; meanwhile the watchman was encouraging me to play on it. With trembling hands I sat down and played one of my original compositions inspired by *Dance of the Sugar Plum Fairy.* The piano felt like butter. It was an antique Euterpe in immaculate condition. I felt history passing beneath my fingertips, and I imagine that my Grandma Marilyn Rasmussen was smiling down from heaven.

The night watchman also gave us a tour of the Milka Chocolate museum right next door, which was adjacent to a castle where knights jousted long ago. He told us that in medieval times this was also a place where open-air puppet theaters went on portraying Bible stories. They were pop-up shows held during jousting tournaments. I had already learned about these types of hand puppets and history at a museum in Budapest many years prior. I even saw puppets that were made to look like Elijah, Moses, angels, demons and other Bible figures—but I had never visited a site where these shows actually took place.

Seeing this castle affirmed to me one of the reasons our shows were so effective in Eastern Europe: we were actually carrying on a long European tradition of telling Bible stories in the streets using puppets. When I developed The Suitcase Sideshow, I had no idea it would be such a nostalgic production for Eastern Europe—something people would love and was already part of their heritage.

Our last show of the tour took place in a town where the entire local church consisted of only four women of prayer. They brought us to a park to perform, and I was a little disappointed and thought, "This isn't really a good place for us. There are just a few people, and it's mostly toddlers." My mind flashed back to the Polish show we did, four years prior, on the Baltic Sea for tourists in the amphitheater, and I knew God had led us here. I just needed to follow His prompting and watch my attitude.

We set up and somehow gathered our largest Ukrainian crowd of the entire tour. Midway through the performance, dark clouds came rolling in, and I prayed that God would keep the rain away. We finished the show and I preached the Gospel faster than I had ever done up to that point. As soon as I finished, downpour began. I yelled, "If anyone wants to know more about God in this way, go under that tree and I'll meet you there."

We grabbed the stage, and in the blinding rain we hastily moved it under the tree. There we found people waiting for us, and some were already talking with members of the local church. I talked to one boy who had seen the show and was wholly moved by how I spoke of God. After a powerful conversation with him and his uncle, they both believed in Jesus that day and prayed to receive Him into their lives.

It was a long process and took a lot of effort to perform in Ukraine, but God led us there at a time when people needed Him the most. We just needed to say yes, not live in fear, and adapt our calling to the family stage of life which we were in—every step of the way. The story continues and we hope for an opportunity for the whole family to go back again someday.

RED - EYE
FLIGHTSOVER
MOSCOW

TOLD BY SARI J. SHOREY

———————•◆•———————

(2007 - 2015)

DURING A NURSING school spring break in 2007 I went on a medical mission trip to Guatemala where I volunteered as a scrub nurse in an operating room. After that experience I decided my life path was headed towards medical work in underserved communities. I thought, to be really useful, I should apply for medical school. I love learning and I love creating art, both bring me joy, but I set aside art because I didn't want it to be a distraction.

A few months later, I graduated from nursing school. I was about to begin a hospital-nursing job, while also continuing my education to become a doctor. However, some cheap plane tickets enticed me to take a spontaneous trip to Europe.

While visiting with friends in Berlin I received that serendipitous email from Philip and was eager to see his performance at Mauerpark. As I waited in anticipation to see a show, I began thinking about my future plans. I knew I would need to rely on God throughout the demands of medical school and residency. Turning to God, to seek Him for strength, I began to ask if this career plan was from me or Him. As I held my future with an open hand He shifted my mind and I knew that I would not need to pursue more education to serve God.

I felt encouraged. I knew this would bring me joy but I had no concept of how it would be useful or how I would find space for art in my life. But I was eager to see how God could use this gift that brought me so much joy.

A few minutes later I met Philip and was freshly open for whatever adventures God had for me. We married in 2009 and a few years later I began working as a school nurse where in the late spring of 2015, I was preparing my health office for summer break. Philip was already engrossed with making final travel arrangements for our summer tour, and when the school year ended I started to make a detailed packing plan for our 10-month baby and 2-year-old toddler. All our belongings needed to fit into one suitcase and I wanted to cram everything necessary to create homey abodes as our family of four traveled through Albania, Poland, and Turkey.

A couple of days before our departure, Philip shared with me that our script had still not been translated into Albanian. My heart sank as I struggled with a longing to be useful and effective. Without having a translation ready to go, we would probably not have a fruitful trip because there would be no show to record or perform. It might be more like a scouting trip or restless vacation. We had already received financial support for this trip and worked jobs nine-months out of the year to pay for our travel and ministry expenses; however, there is also a cost of time and effort that must be met by a local and committed team. If locals are not passionate or inspired by the project, our presence may not change anything and we could even be an inconvenience or burden to them.

Just as our plans for Albania were folding, our friend in Turkey unexpectedly requested that we go to Kyrgyzstan to trail blaze a partnership there. I had my handwritten packing list but an altered itinerary required more preparation. I began researching Kyrgyzstan's history, weather, clothing, diet, and the CDC's guidelines for visitors. My research lead me to a thrift store for a few long skirts and to the doctor's office for a vaccine for our youngest son. Then I headed to the pharmacy because I am allergic to lamb and one of the main proteins on the Kyrgyz menu is mutton. I wanted to refill my prescription for an epinephrine pen before our departure, but the cost was so high that I settled on bringing my slightly expired injector. I expected to struggle with feeling unprepared, but somehow I shrugged it off because I was in the mood for an adventure.

We had never imagined going to Kyrgyzstan but we felt intrigued and excited by the prospect of going further east. The show was already translated into Russian, and our friend from Turkey said the people there were flexible and ready with performance ideas. Kyrgyzstan is situated in the most unreached area of the world and is crossed by the Silk Road between China and Jerusalem. It was part of the former Soviet Union and is frequently in flux over its alliance to Russia, economic loyalty to the United States, and aid from Turkish Islamic missionaries. It is a stew pot of Slavic, Islamic, and Asian cultures with the predominant languages being Russian and Kyrgyz.

Midway through our European tour Philip flew from Ukraine and I flew from Bulgaria with our two boys and my mother. We all met on a layover in Moscow. Our kids were overwhelmed with the joy of seeing their papa and we showered Philip with kisses. We wanted to catch up on the past week and eat some traditional Russian food, but had to settle on fish and chips from an Irish pub as we discussed the uncertainties about the next part of the tour. A few days earlier, on the headline news, the Kyrgyz government had ceremoniously denounced a treaty with the United States over a dispute about the genocide of the Uzbeks in 2005. We were uncertain about the extent of the disagreement and if Kyrgyzstan could spontaneously require visas for Americans.

After three delays, the five of us finally boarded our sleepless five-hour flight to Bishkek, Kyrgyzstan and when we landed just before 6 am—it was stunningly warm. I was dripping with sweat while bouncing an overtired/over-stimulated infant in a carrier on my chest. I started questioning my sanity, but tried to assure myself it was just sleep deprivation. As we waited in the crowded customs line, I promised to sleep the moment my children were snug in their car seats.

Our hosts were waiting for us at the exit of the airport and were welcoming. Their pleasant humor defined much of our time together. Philip hopped into what he thought was the passenger side of the car, but discovered there was a steering wheel. My research never mentioned that vehicles in Kyrgyzstan have steering wheels on either side. I began to wonder what else would surprise me on this tour.

As we drove to our rented flat, I no longer cared about sleeping—I was falling in love with this beautiful country as I watched the city awaken and I didn't want to miss a thing. I saw elderly women sweeping the streets in front of their shops housed in converted shipping containers. Young women in traditional Kyrgyz garments were selling fermented horse milk from barrel-shaped beverage dispensers on every corner (which is the national beverage and incredibly healthy for your gut). Aged farmers were perched upon wagons overflowing with ripe watermelons. There were lush trees lining boulevards and every architectural structure appeared to be constructed out of concrete or corrugated metal. In America this would have been modern and trendy, but here it was simply practical and available.

We settled into our flat in a typical communist housing block and made a quick trip to the grocery store. Our next task was to perform the show for our hosts, so they would fully understand what we could offer.

After we presented our show that day our new friends were very eager to utilize us and one man expressed that he was shocked that something so small could be the vehicle for such a big message. Our new friends were *also* bold messengers of the gospel; however, they were hesitant to use the show in the public squares because there had been a growing ISIS network developing underground, and the KGB was working with the Kyrgyz government to take it down. A conflict between the police and the terrorist group was all over the Kyrgyz news. Seven ISIS members were killed in the clash resulting in increased tension in the country. Our team discerned it would be better to keep the show in private institutions since it was in Russian.

Our schedule for the week quickly filled with two shows per day in orphanages and nursing homes around Bishkek. Everyday my saintly mother stayed at our flat to watch Axel and Casper. It took a lot of effort for me to arrange their daily activities, meals, pump milk for bottle feeding, and then set out with Philip for a day packed with shows, travel, and ministry. At night we'd return to jet lagged babies who wanted an entire day's worth of my attention crammed into an evening, only to do it all over again the next day. Yet I felt like each day was more of a special dating adventure with Philip than work and was refreshed with laughter.

Humor was constant while we were in Kyrgyzstan. Five of us squished into a mini-van with the marionettes and stage.We jokingly made far-fetched business plans about selling Kyrgyz yurts in America to fund missionaries. Sarcasm is rarely effective cross-culturally, but in Kyrgyzstan it never let up.

After one of the first shows in an orphanage, many of the kids eagerly raised their hands wanting to know Jesus. Several of the workers already followed Jesus and had been teaching the kids about the love of God; we were simply part of the harvest. At another orphanage, the workers were really touched by the message and we prayed this would affect the kids like we'd seen elsewhere. We were starting to see why God had changed our plans.

We often explain to others that while the marionettes draw a younger crowd, our *Blessed are the Poor* production is geared for more mature audiences; however, we see kids get a lot from the show, even though it has some pretty heavy content. Nevertheless, during this trip we began to strongly desire to travel with a production for all-ages. When we returned to

Minneapolis, we prioritized this and developed a story called *The Sailor and the Boat.*

Whenever we travel, we are intentional to allow extra time between performances so that we can truly learn about where we are. After many of our shows in the orphanages of Kyrgyzstan, we played Ping-Pong, filled water balloons, played soccer, and taught the Singing Saw. We have learned to let our tours move at a slower pace, which allows time to see life from other perspectives, and experience the culture—even if it gets a little uncomfortable.

After one show Philip was invited over to the pool for some male bonding time. He had just had a pretty low experience at an outhouse (which had become commonplace for us because of the bacteria in the food that our western microbiomes were adjusting to). It probably would have been wise to avoid swimming, but they were urging him over. He later told me, "All the guys were swimming and insisting I jump in but I didn't have any swim shorts." He felt hesitant and confided in the host, "You know, to publicly swim in my underwear isn't part of my culture." The host replied, "Yes I know, but here in Kyrgyzstan you can be free." Philip had a brief crisis and had to assess if it was moral or cultural. Then within a few minutes he was getting really wet and having a moment of cultural integration for the sake of the Gospel.

I wish I could be an immediate cultural expert through research, but I have had to learn that there are no shortcuts to discovering cultural cues. An important practice is to just be present and only when the time is right, ask questions. Time, a desire to learn, a willingness to take risks, releasing control, and humility helps me down the path towards cultural competency. If I have knowledge of a country's Wikipedia page but am always in a hurry, I will trample cultural norms leaving no opportunity for feedback, growth, and grace.

During this time in Kyrgyzstan I also faced a cultural dilemma. My mother and I observed oppression and experienced the frequent exclusion of females. Of course I was already aware and passionate about the unjust treatment of women throughout the world, but here in Kyrgystan I was becoming consumed in a mental battle. I lovingly tried to formulate how I could empower Kyrgyz women and improve their autonomy but at the same time a voice in my head started to question if I was perpetuating the situation by appearing to be a dutiful wife who was following my husband's calling. This thought surprised me because I know that the calling is just as much my own. I asked God to help me put aside my cynicism and fight against my heart becoming defensive. He reminded me that Christ is an amazing defender of the oppressed and that He highly values women. I witnessed that Christians in Kyrgyzstan stand against this part of their culture and also recognize that men and women were both created in the image of God and deserve fair treatment. This is revolutionary in a country like Kyrgyzstan where the act of bride kidnapping[27] is still practiced. When we seek to love like Christ, that love has the power to deconstruct class systems, racial oppression, and gender inequality.

On the third day of the tour we headed towards a nursing home where our driver nearly ran over an elderly blind man walking down the driveway. After the van haphazardly parked, we were led to a small auditorium. As I was setting up the marionettes, Philip began playing a favorite melody (Bubamara) on the accordion to help set the atmosphere. To our surprise the blind man appeared and burst out singing the lyrics to this traditional folk song at the top of his lungs in Serbian. Through a translator he shared that he loved this song and that it was written by a Serbian Roma. The blind man went and grabbed his accordion and played a duet with Philip. Their music drew many more people to our show and we were asked to relocate to a larger lounge downstairs. We carried our stage there and they continued playing more music together.

---

27 A marriage practice where a man, with the help of his friends, kidnap his love interest or a woman off the street and bring her to an already prepared wedding. His family convinces her to marry him. This act is illegal, but it is still common in rural areas where the police don't know it's illegal, or just don't care because it is tradition.

After shuffling some sofas and maneuvering a few wheelchairs, it was time to begin. Philip warned the audience, "There are some sad, funny, and scary parts because it is a story about life." He later told me he didn't want anyone to die of shock or have a heart attack during the show—our audience *did* appear quite frail. After the show, he shared the Gospel and many people responded. Some even overcame trembling hands and outstretched both arms as they prayed to ask Jesus into their lives.

Philip and I approached a woman who had seemed very engaged in our show and she burst into tears. We didn't know her full story but she wouldn't let go of our hands. While Philip prayed with her, our new blind friend started playing a Christmas hymn on his accordion as if he was the musical accompaniment in a church service.

Philip was invited to the blind man's room because he wanted to show Philip how he can operate a computer. I remained downstairs to pack up the puppets, since I was eager to return to my babies. He told Philip that he was a Christian and that he had been blind his whole life. He prayed over Philip. Philip then declared to him, "Someday we will see each other with Jesus. We will understand one another's language and play accordion music together as worship to our Lord."

Accordionists have been maligned by comics about harps being in heaven and accordions exclusively for hell, but Philip and his friend were quite certain there will be accordion music in heaven too. I am very excited to hear them play together again and you are all invited to worship God with us.

The next performance was a long drive from Bishkek. On the way there we drove parallel to the ancient Silk Road and a local team member pointed out archeological sites where the Apostle Thomas spread the Gospel across Asia and into India around 52 AD. The Kyrgyz Muslim government was working to cover them up but we trusted our team's astonishing insight on the tough issues pertaining to Islam and Christianity as most were former Muslims themselves.

We drove a couple of hours and arrived at a Muslim-run nursing home on the foothills of the Chinese High Mountains. There were five hundred people living in the gated concrete facility and about one hundred came to see our show. During the show, everyone on our team noticed two workers with very stern expressions glaring at us. I thought for sure we were in trouble, especially when Philip took the message all the way and asked people who wanted to know Jesus to raise their hands and pray. He figured if the workers were upset about the show—and if we were going to get shut down, he wanted it to be for something worthwhile. My own motherly thoughts were "If we get kicked out, maybe I will return to my kids earlier."

Then many people raised their hands and even more prayed with us. Then one of the stern-looking workers walked over and took the microphone from Philip. I thought, "Here we go, we're done. I hope the people who raised their hands don't get in trouble." But instead of reprimanding us, the worker expressed his appreciation for the message by publicly thanking us for coming. He was a Muslim, but said he was happy that we were there because many of these people will die very soon and needed God. We were flooded with relief and sensed the Holy Spirit at work.

We stayed at the facility for lunch and fellowship. While we dined on horse soup, our friends and hosts expressed awe over the fact that we were a family with small kids willing to set aside our "American comforts" to travel with them. I responded with a blasé remark, "Most people could do it if they would just plan and be organized." This comment resulted in uproarious laughter from our new friends who joyfully informed me that I was covered by God's grace and unaware of the degree of strength afforded to me. In that moment, I recognized that even my ability to prepare and consent to this trip was coming from God and not my own determination.

On our last day in Kyrgyzstan, we celebrated all that God

had done throughout the week. We visited the mountains and had dinner in a yurt surrounded by God's majestic creation and our new friends. We enjoyed traditional drinks, fresh caught trout from a river, and watched as Axel laughed and danced while wearing a traditional Kyrgyz hat. We all hoped to work together again and planned that during our next visit we will travel amongst the nomads to perform our show in yurts throughout the countryside. At nightfall we drove down the mountain, gathered our luggage, and boarded our flight from Bishkek, Kyrgyzstan to Istanbul, Turkey.

We were midway through our red-eye flight when the interior lights were abruptly illuminated. The flight attendants rushed to the front of the plane and in three languages they requested the assistance of a doctor as an emergency medical situation arose in first class. No one moved. Then they pleaded for a nurse. Everyone remained still and silent as I counted to three and waited for someone more qualified to respond. However, I was the only healthcare worker present. I unlatched my nursing baby, passed Casper to Philip, and hurried to the front of the airplane. In the aisle near the first row, a woman was lying supine with the pilot and flight attendants hovering over her. The staff parted as I approached and identified myself as a nurse. I got on my knees beside her to check for a pulse and tipped her head back to open her airway while my words were translated from person to person. Then the pilot spoke to me in a language I did not recognize. My patient began spontaneously breathing as the pilot's translated words reached me. "Do I need to land the plane in Pakistan?" I vigorously rubbed my patient's sternum and shook her shoulders. She revived consciousness and the flight attendants translated my patient's language into another and then into Russian and finally into English.

I learned very confusing information about her medical history but continued assessing her by checking her blood pressure and temperature using supplies from a medical bag on board. I stayed with her as her color returned and her breathing became unlabored. She appeared stable and we agreed it was unnecessary to interrupt the flight and land. The pilot and staff profusely thanked me as I returned to my seat. All eyes were on me as I stepped through the curtain separating first class from my assigned row near the back of the plane. I gave an assuring nod to the passengers and there were audible sighs of relief throughout the plane.

After I sat down and resumed feeding Casper I was flooded with gratitude and felt seen and loved by God. This moment was like a gift because it spoke to my longing to feel tangibly effective and use the other talents that He gave me. At times I have laid that desire aside out of obedience, but I felt very useful in Kyrgyzstan and was the only person equipped to help this woman and keep us en route during another red-eye flight.

BETWEEN A MOSQUE AND A STARBUCKS

TOLD BY PHILIP SHOREY

(2006 - 2015)

I TOURED WITH No Longer Music for the first time in 2006. Throughout this tour I lugged audio recording gear with me and took every opportunity to record my marionette show into new languages. Then in early July, No Longer Music performed in Germany at Freak Stock Festival on the main stage during opening night. I remember close to one hundred people responded to the message given after the show. I was able to pray with three or four people and was thrilled and encouraged to see God move so mightily. Then we all enjoyed the festival—playing foosball, going to shows, and even playing soccer before our journey east to Turkey. The last day before we departed we were asked to clean up and help take down the festival.

It was raining but we knew if we kept working we'd stay warm, so we began to disassemble a huge circus tent, and as we did, I was drawn into a conversation with a girl named Anna.

She had seen the No Longer Music show, but was terrified of it. She wanted to know Jesus, but was scared of what might happen to her if she took that step. She spent most of her remaining time at the festival trying to fight the battle out on her own, while hiding in her tent and getting lost in the woods. She wanted to meet someone from NLM and ask several questions, so while standing there in the cold rain, we talked for a couple hours as I explained the Gospel to her. I told her that the train had not left, and we could pray right here in the rain if she truly wanted to receive Jesus into her life. She finally said, "Yes" and as we prayed she began to cry and we both felt a warm wind of God completely wrap His arms around her. It was one of the most beautiful things I had ever witnessed. Anna was ecstatic! She began to tell other people who were helping break down the tent, and a huge celebration happened as people prayed and thanked God for revealing Himself to her. I was privileged to be part of what her friends had already been doing to reach out to her all along, and now God had used me and NLM to help her take the next big step of faith.

That night, I went to bed up in a tower overlooking a racehorse track with the rest of the band and was feeling so blessed. The next morning I woke up after a chilly night and felt a little queasy. I skipped breakfast and got in the van with the band as we made our journey along Germany's legendary Autobahn, reaching speeds of 150 mph. We arrived at the airport and began to wait for our boarding call.

Without going into too much detail, I ended up puking on a number of occasions throughout the German airport. Thankfully the flight was uneventful, but as I was getting my visa to enter Turkey, I vomited again, this time all over my friend Nate's legs. This happened right in front of the border patrol officer, and in front of the passport window just as a huge bus full of tourists were arriving from Barcelona.

This was bitter sweet. Bitter, because I felt ill and Nate wasn't too happy with me. Sweet, because this was my first time entering a Muslim country and I was really nervous about choosing what to say to persuade them to let me in. But after I made a mess of the floor, officers just stamped my passport, issued me a visa, and rushed me to the bathroom with no questions asked. God works in mysterious ways.

Our team reconvened and I was shown to the place we were

staying and went straight to bed. I had some kind of stomach virus and had to sit out the next day.

As I was recovering in bed I began to think back to why I had gotten sick. Maybe I got sick because travelling had worn down my immune system, and the day before I was standing in the rain for hours without a jacket, telling someone about Jesus. Here was a girl that almost slipped between the cracks who had now found a new life in such a powerful way. All I had to do was go through a day or two of suffering, but what was my suffering in comparison to what Jesus did for her and what she had just been saved from?

Instead of dwelling on my sickness, I actually felt an overwhelming sense of purpose come over me, as I knew Jesus could use me if I was willing. I heard Jesus say, "This is what I have called you to do, but are you willing to suffer more than just vomiting in both Europe and Asia in one day for my name?" I don't need to tell the world all the details about the conversations I have with my Lord, but I think this is a good question for everybody that knows Jesus to ask. That is why I pose the following question as I tell this story. Jesus suffered on a cross so that we may know His love, so how much are you willing to suffer so that others may know God's love? I have seen that many things of value only happen after a struggle, and oftentimes spiritual and physical attacks follow powerful acts of God; however, be encouraged: truth wins, and all of it is nothing in comparison to the joys ahead.

We continued our No Longer Music tour that year, and it was also a huge trailblazing year for The Suitcase Sideshow. Along the way I met the man who organized much of the NLM tour. We became close friends and I was able to share with him the vision of my traveling marionette theater. He told me that they had been praying for someone to come work with them in the use of puppets to reach Muslims for Jesus. We clicked and began the process of translating our *Blessed are the Poor* show into Turkish.

We created a modern day story about Jesus (Isa as written in the Quran) coming to the Turkish Muslim world today. It felt like a tightrope walk, because Jesus is seen as a prophet to Muslims, but they don't really know much about Him. We created a show that would be for Turks, by Turks, and would reveal the love of God through three modernized Bible stories set in Turkey today.

In 2010, Sari and I returned to Turkey with The Suitcase Sideshow. It was the last stop on our six-month long tour, and we had traveled through much of Eastern Europe and had seen God move so much. We were excited for this new challenge of sharing Christ in a Muslim culture through our antique marionettes. Our first task was to work and rework the soundtrack to make sure it was just right.

After our first show, people thought it was a satirical performance and we knew we still needed to tweak a lot of the details. We had a Turkish voice actor rerecord Jesus' voice to sound more sincere. This new voice actor was a former Muslim who had been in jail a few times for his faith in Jesus. He was a born Turk, had become a TV actor, and later a street vendor. After he reworked the lines, the show was significantly improved. His theatrical contribution really conveyed the spirit of God's love for us, and the people who watched the show could tell that it was earnest. Covered Turkish women were seen crying during the prostitute scene, other people had questions and some people wanted to know more. Debates between crowd members were stirred up, we engaged in a game of cat and mouse: discerning between the secret police, and those who really wanted to see the show and understand it.

In my previous visit to Turkey with No Longer Music, I had felt this looming sense of fear at all times, like the "Eye of Sauron" from *The Lord of the Rings* was watching us and plotting against us. I would wake up hearing the Muslim call to prayer in the middle of the night, reminding me where I was, reminding the nation what it should believe. The jolt from peaceful sleep would send me into a whirl of thoughts; I even became physically sick at times. I would not feel this form of anxiety again until 2021 when I would drive Sari and Axel (age 8) into Mexico during the Coronavirus Pandemic to preach the Gospel in the parks with The Suitcase Sideshow.

But something changed in me on this visit to Turkey. I wasn't afraid anymore. I wasn't even afraid to go to jail. My wife can testify to that, which made her quite nervous—but God was also working in her heart by building her boldness and love for Turkey through a beautiful book by Lenna Lidstone (*You Will See Hoopoes*) and opportunities to see where Florence Nightingale (founder of modern nursing) served during the Crimean War.

I don't know if what transpired in me was a better understanding of the country's law, or if the Holy Spirit had given me what I needed to be bold in Turkey—but I had so much fun through openly proclaiming the Gospel of Jesus in a place that is known for open persecution and even death to the church. The team we were with was also amazing, encouraging, and bold.

There is little in comparison to the camaraderie of preaching the good news with other passionate people, and this is a real testimony of how Jesus living inside a person can change a person's outlook. It's like we could feel angels protecting us. People always look at me as if I'm crazy to visit Turkey with the intentions of openly sharing. The more unstable the Middle East situation gets, and the more children I have, the crazier people think I am—but I have a wild peace that passes my understanding and some really good contacts there who are smart as well as bold. In situations like this, Christianity isn't passive and boring, it's active and alive! I love that. That's just how I remember discovering Jesus for the first time growing up in the camper doing "Kids' Crusades," and that's how Christianity is suppose to be—untamed and unspoiled by religion.

One afternoon, we set up our show in a plaza on the more conservative side of Istanbul. We wanted to do at least two shows each day and so attempting a daytime show was normal. We didn't have much of a crowd, but the longer we performed the more of a crowd we attracted. As we performed, one audience member approached us and said something in Turkish. I didn't understand him and just kept my focus on performing. One of our helpers who is fluent in Turkish started talking to him. They got into a heated discussion and our friends told us to stop and start packing up right away because this man had called the police. The moment we paused the soundtrack the audience began yelling at him and saying, "If this show is for God, let it continue. If it is for politics, let it stop." Most of the people still wanted to see the rest of the show, but couldn't because of the loud voice of one.

We were still hurriedly packing up as the police arrived. They spoke to my translator, and while they were talking, someone I didn't know, (but later learned was a local Christian) snuck up behind me and quietly whispered, "Whatever you say, don't let them call you a missionary."

The word "missionary" carries a lot of negative or political innuendos in many cultures—and this is the case in Turkey. When you look at the historical or cultural context of missionaries in a specific culture, you can start to see where their misconceptions come from. Islamic missionaries from Turkey go all over the world and are funded by Turkish tax-dollars with a political agenda to spread Islam. I have seen this firsthand in Kyrgyzstan where there are multi-million dollar Turkish mosques and Islamic schools being built. Islamic Turkish missionaries sponsor the Kyrgyz government to build "public" universities, schools, and mosques with Turkish wealth if they can teach Islam publicly and forbid other religions. As they do this their religion grows. Subsequently, the Turkish people and police assume that the American government, with a western political agenda, fund missionaries as well—but we know that couldn't be further from the truth.

We receive no government funding. Those who believe in what we do and want to partner through prayer and fundraising support us. We also use our own finances when needed. Our missions work feels very grassroots and connected to the greater body of believers. Turks usually hate that their taxes go to fund Islamic missionaries while the people would rather use it to better their own lives, infrastructure, and economic growth. How interesting is this, that in Christianity we have to convince people to support missions and sometimes even convince people that supporting missionaries is okay, but in Islam, the government supports missionaries. In much of the Middle East, politics and religion are the same. Thank God, that for us, missions is not a game of numbers and money, but a movement of truth and love.

Finally the police spoke to me directly. They were convinced we were government funded missionaries and they asked us for our passports. Sari didn't have hers with her, which made the officers very upset. They scolded me and told me to keep my wife in check as they sent her away to go get it. By some miracle, they let us go—but threatened me with jail if they ever saw us doing this again.

The next evening we did the show again, but across the city on the more liberal side. We found a bustling place to set up where lots of locals and tourists from all over the Middle East strolled by. We started performing the show adjacent to other street performers, and once in a while a few police officers would walk by and do nothing. Then a couple policemen walked towards us, but they were just on their way to Starbucks. We finished the whole show, and it seemed like a real victory. There was even one man who said he had seen the beginning of the show the previous day on the more conservative side of the city. The very show that had been shut down. He wanted to see the whole thing but couldn't because of the scene that one man had made. Now here, in a city of over 14 million, he had found us on the opposite side of the city. He came to faith in Jesus that day.

As we did many other shows in those couple weeks, they all went so well that the local group we were working with began to believe that this should continue on a regular basis. During the following spring of 2011 we returned to Turkey with another set of marionettes and a steamer trunk which the team in Turkey fabricated into their own traveling marionette street theater. We taught a group how to perform the show, and spent a week teaching and preparing them for this new method of evangelistic street performing. Just as I learned from my family how to share Christ through puppets, the tradition was being passed on to more brothers and sisters in *faith*, not *blood*.

At the end of the week, we took the new stage and team out to the streets and let the new puppet troupe take a step of faith in performing this radical show of God's love through Isa (Jesus) themselves. The first show was alright. It wasn't the ideal place to perform, but we had a few good talks and the team didn't get into any trouble. The second show was in the shadow of a giant mosque. We weren't sure how the location would affect things, but as I watched the crowd listen, my heart was touched. This was a fairly big crowd, and many people stayed and were fully engaged by the whole show, while others pretended they weren't interested—but they still couldn't help but stick around out of curiosity.

There was one businessman in front who didn't move the entire show. After the show was over, he approached one of the performers and said, "This show was amazing! Islam is old and doesn't relate to modern life. But these stories are real and I relate to this. I feel spiritually empty. I need this. Please don't leave me. I need to know more about this."

The Suitcase Sideshow 2.0 has toured Turkey and Bulgaria for many years. They have seen people express interest in Jesus countless times. They meet with people who are interested and work with them to understand this newfound love of God in a radical way.

In 2015, we were honored to return as a family of four (plus Sari's mom to help with the kids) and retrain and encourage the fourth team of performers there that have been so faithful and have sacrificed so much to continue to spread the message of

Jesus in such a high-risk and unstable part of the world. To me they are real rock stars.

I love Turkey. I love the culture, street food, excitement, spirit of creativity, and their orange juice. I loved sharing the orange juice with my son. It's like a natural Everlasting Gobstopper from Willy Wonka and the Chocolate Factory. The flavor literally changes three times in your mouth. The history of this region of the world gives me a sense of connection with the timeless Church, because so many efforts of the early church were spent doing what we are doing in the exact same places. I love the people, and the fact that their nightlife doesn't involve getting drunk. I love the teashop atmosphere and the old men playing backgammon in the streets. Axel loves the street cats and we all love the ferry rides with the most breathtaking views in the world. I love a good Turkish shave. And most of all I love the feeling of excitement that comes with sharing the truth of Jesus with many people who I believe are looking for God in their lives, but reject The Way (Jesus) because of misunderstandings and western misrepresentation. Turkey and the people who serve in Turkey are forever in my prayers.

PHOTOS

Philip and Patches

Philip and Sari get married

Philip and Sari with Noah and Wendy on tour

Street performance in Poland

Performing at the Polish amphitheatre

Philip and Sari perform at SLOT

Woodstock Poland

Performing in Ukraine

At an orphanage in Kyrgyzstan

Philip, Sari, Axel, and Casper in Kyrgyzstan

There will be accordions in heaven

Axel in Kyrgyzstan

Celebrating with horse meat in Kyrgyzstan

Philip and Sari walking to their show in Istanbul

Sari hides behind the stage before performing in Turkey

Axel falls in love with the street cats of Istanbul

The Turkish Suitcase Sideshow performs

The Suitcase Sideshow 2.0 performs in Istanbul

Sari on the ferry in Istanbul

Family of five heads to Europe in 2018

Philip and Sari

EPILOGUE

MANY PEOPLE DESIRE a sense of belonging and seek a connection to something greater than themselves. Reflecting on the historical moments in this book has given me an opportunity to look back and process the purpose, legacy, and role family has in society. There have been times that I deeply wished to be more like members of my own family. I looked up to my relatives and wanted God to use me as he had used them in their generation. Then other times, I have gratitude for the unique calling on my own life. Now I have come full circle with children of my own, and recognize the tension that can exist between a generational blessing and the fallibility of human family. I wish to conclude with the following thoughts:

What we do right now will not only affect our own lives, but generations to come. For some, that reality is a blessing, for others, a curse; however, it's never too late to ignite a blessing, one that will last and leave a legacy that will outlive its generation and continue to impact the world. The sacrifice and challenge is to let go of our own pride and comfort and know that Jesus was who he said he was, and turn from selfishness, self-righteousness, arrogance, and shame, to ask, "Jesus, what is it you want me to do?"

At the same time, I realize that whether we receive a curse or a blessing from previous generations, we are neither bound nor set free by our past. "I press on toward the goal for the prize of the upward call of God in Christ Jesus" (Philippians 3:14). The goal should never be to imitate others in your family, or anyone for that matter. The goal is to be the best YOU version of Jesus that YOU can be. There is freedom in that—freedom that you are not bound or destined to the same end as your family—

freedom that you do not have to carry a generational burden. There is no pressure for you to live up to any past standard or dream. You have a path made uniquely for you. That path includes an invitation to be a part of his family. Although the past can influence the future, it does not predict it.

On the surface, puppets have appeared as the hallmark of creative methods throughout this generational book, but the true inheritance has been the theme of killing your art, dreams, and own plans for how you will achieve success in your life and surrendering it all to God. "Truly, truly, I say to you, unless a grain of wheat falls into the earth and dies, it remains alone; but if it dies, it bears much fruit (John 12-24 ESV)."

John Shorey answered this call when he gave up marksmanship and Marilyn Rasmussen when she gave up figure skating. I too experienced moments of surrender—most notably when I quit soccer and again upon returning to college from Brazil after I performed my show in the brothel. Instead of pursuing the rat-race and trying to make it as a composer in Hollywood, I knew what I wanted to really do was change the world. So maybe, in an upside down kind of way, to take my art to the street, kill it, and allow God to use my simple puppet show was to make a bigger difference than composing music for a film that would probably be lost and forgotten about. After all, the world doesn't need another blockbuster film, the world needs Jesus!

Ever since I waived my opportunity to have a film scoring internship in 2005 I have not sought to return to a composition career. Then in the fall of 2016, Sari and I were given some tickets to go see Nosferatu – A Symphony of Horror (1922) which is an old silent film. It was featured at the Parkway Theater in Minneapolis and accompanied by a seven-piece ensemble. The show was good and the music was fun, but the way the group interpreted the film through the music didn't sit right with me. The vampire was kind of creepy in a funny way, and the woman who gave her life to destroy the vampire was portrayed as a damsel in distress.

I had fallen in love with this film back in high school and

seeing it again made me reminiscent of the Philip Glass score to Dracula with the Kronos Quartet which was the initial album that lead me to fall in love with film music. Then I remembered the moment in college when Nosferatu brought me to tears as I witnessed the allegorical imagery of the Gospel displayed through the powerful and loving sacrifice of the lead female character. I sensed I had to do something with that film someday.

It was at that moment, sitting in the Parkway Theater, not fully satisfied with the lens this composer had written the music through, that I felt God speak to me again and say, "Okay then, NOW...do something with it."

I prayed about it and took a mental inventory of the resources and skills I had. I knew if the project involved music it would need to be big to convey the power of the love force that overcame the strength of the vampire's terror. Over the years I dabbled in creating musical themes for it on my accordion and invited friends over on cold autumn nights to watch the film projected on the back of my house as I would perform under a full moon around a campfire in my yard... but for something like this I would need an orchestra and I didn't have one. My suitcase theater didn't seem right and a vampire marionette show was a little too cliché; too much "creepy." I began to consider a new creative direction and discovered a Brazilian artist with a gift for gothic cartooning. We worked together and developed a comic book called "Curse of the Vampire."

Something was driving me to do this very quickly. I just couldn't stop. My wife got annoyed with me as I struggled to balance family, work, and this new project. She knows me as a minister and music lover, but not a comic book author. She was befuddled by this new hobby that I had never had any inkling of prior passion for and she insisted, "If you want to do something with Nosferatu, you should be writing music for it." I would reply, "Of course I want to, but I don't have an orchestra." She went away and prayed about it, and God gave her total peace about it and told her, "If this is from Philip it will stop, but if it is from me, he won't be able to stop it, so don't try to stop him."

The comic book morphed into an unconventional tract that

would draw readers into a timeless vampire story that includes many parallel points to the Gospel. Then at the conclusion of the fictional story I shared the inspiration for the art and described the true and powerful way that Jesus sacrificed his life for us and defeated death. We handed the comic books out at Marilyn Manson shows, Zombie Pub Crawls, metal shows, and vampire raves.

Then one day I was in Germany chatting with one of the directors of SLOT Art Festival. I mentioned the comic book to her, and suggested that she show Nosferatu and hand this comic book out at their festival. She agreed, but then said, "If we show Nosferatu, it would need live music because it is a silent film. Could you write music for it?" I was shocked. I took a deep breath and gulped. I said, "Yes..." and knowing the amount of work that would take to compose wall-to-wall orchestral music for a 95-minute silent film (approximately 4hrs for every minute of film = 475hrs), I tried to reason with her about how impractical it was and shared what my biggest reservation would be, "But I don't have an orchestra." She replied that the festival had a volunteer orchestra that I could use and they would feature me as an "up-and-coming" composer so I could perform my music to Nosferatu. I told her, "I would need to be able to share the Gospel at the end," to which she responded, "I would expect nothing less."

I was in shock as I recognized that God had seen my faithfulness with the little things, and was now entrusting me with a larger platform to reach the masses. At that moment I soberly acknowledged that the temptations will be greater, and I must never forget that I am still just a street performer. I treasure the Kill Your Art lessons on success, identity, priorities, and humility learned in the streets as an evangelistic street performer because if I forget about them, I'm dead. I have also realized that my God believed in me, and that my story was not over, it was just beginning. We named this new project the Curse of the Vampire Orchestra and have gathered volunteer orchestras and performed across the globe. We have seen hundreds publicly take a step towards Christ after our shows who are now starting generational blessings.

We all have a choice to form a legacy within a godly faith, or humanistic faith. Although, there is a lot of wisdom we can glean from previous generations, no other person, not even a former family member, is worthy to be placed on a pedestal as an idol. Only Jesus deserves our praise!

We all make mistakes and our stories are still being written. There is still time to change. Even as I reflect on the stories shared here, I realize any blessing shared in my own family wasn't because of our own achievements, hard work, or talents accomplished on his or her own. Rather, the amazing things that happened were because of obedience to God and his mercy and power working through us, or even in spite of us at times. He is such a loving dad. If we lose sight of that truth and stumble into pride over our own accomplishments, we've lost every treasure worth remembering.

Today we travel all over the world and proclaim the good news of Jesus Christ in creative ways, sometimes with the whole family, and sometimes without–always being flexible to prayerfully consider each situation. Maybe one day, the marionettes will be retired again and wait in an attic for the next willing heart to take up that adventure, or maybe we will continue to see God move us in a totally new direction of creative proclamation. One thing is for sure – "...as for me and my household, we will serve the LORD" (Joshua 24:15).

Will you?

APPENDIX

CONTACT

Philip Shorey

Author, Founder, and Director of The Suitcase
Sideshow & Curse of the Vampire Orchestra.

The Suitcase Sideshow
www.suitcasesideshow.org
Curse of the Vampire Orchestra
www.curseofthevampire.com

Other titles by Philip Shorey

Kill Your Art - A Street Performer's Guide to Being a
Messenger of Jesus Christ

Curse of the Vampire - Comic Book

WORKS CITED

[a] "Sideshow World." Jan. 2018, www.sideshowworld.com.

[b] "Emigration From Denmark." Jan. 2018, www.mydanishroots.com.

[c] Conklin Thomas, The Titanic Sinks. Random House Press, 1997.

[d] "Laurentic (I)" 2007, www.whitestarhistory.com.

[e] "History of the FCM." Jan. 2018, www.fcm.org.

[f] "Spasmodic Torticollis - Science Direct 2011, www.sciencedirect.com.

[g] "Musical Saws - About Us." Jan 2018, www.musicalsaws.com.

[h] Seifrit, Brian & Townsend, Alison, A Bloodstained Hammer, CreateSpace Independent Publishing Platform, 2013. 207.

[i] Lymbery, Tom, Tom's Gray Creek A Kootenay Lake Memoir Part 1: Early Years to 1945, Gray Creek Publishing, 2013, p.91.

[j] Drimmer, Frederick. Very Special People, Amjon Publishers, 1985.

[k] "Freaks (1932)." Jan 2018, www.imdb.com/title/tt0022913.

[l] Fonseca, Isabel. Bury Me Standing: The Gypsies and Their Journey. Vintage Departments, 1995, pp. 72, 83- 112.

[m] Pierce, David. Rock Priest. Steiger, 1995, pp. 72, 83- 112.

[n] "John Harper's Last Convert." 2012, www.moodymedia.org.

Made in the USA
Columbia, SC
08 November 2021

48567100R00157